# WILL I GO BLIND?
## LIVING WITH MACULAR DEGENERATION

*Other Books by Noel Mansfield*
*published by Coventry Press*

Dawn to Dusk, Towards a Spirituality of Ageing

LIVING WITH
MACULAR DEGENERATION

# WILL I GO BLIND?

NOEL MANSFIELD, MSC

COVENTRY
PRESS

Published in Australia by
Coventry Press
33 Scoresby Road
Bayswater VIC 3153

ISBN 9781922589101

Copyright © Noel Mansfield MSC 2021

All rights reserved. Other than for the purposes and subject to the conditions prescribed under the *Copyright Act*, no part of this publication may be reproduced, stored in a retrieval system, or transmitted in any form or by any means, electronic, mechanical, photocopying, recording or otherwise, without the prior permission of the publisher.

Scripture taken from the Holy Bible NEW INTERNATIONAL VERSION®, NIV®, Copyright © 1973, 1978, 1984, 2011 by Biblica, Inc.® Used by permission. All rights reserved worldwide.

Catalogue-in-Publication entry is available from the National Library of Australia http://catalogue.nla.gov.au

Cover design by Ian James – www.jgd.com.au
Cover and text photographs by Kenji Konda, MSC
Text design by Coventry Press
Set in Atkinson Hyperlegible (Braille Foundation)

Printed in Australia

# Contents

List of photographs ..................... 7
Foreword .............................. 8
About the author ...................... 11
Acknowledgments ..................... 12
Introduction:
     Disability and marginalisation ...... 14
Chapter 1
     Beginning my story .............. 31
Chapter 2
     Disease and degeneration ....... 45
Chapter 3
     The moment of diagnosis ........ 52
Chapter 4
     The first ophthalmologist ........ 58
Chapter 5
     The second ophthalmologist ........ 71

Chapter 6
    Complications .................. 87

Chapter 7
    Learning Braille ................ 93

Chapter 8
    My substitute for Braille ........ 111

Chapter 9
    Blindness ...................... 116

Chapter 10
    Technical support .............. 130

Chapter 11
    Some questions ................ 144

Chapter 12
    Diet for AMD (Age-related
    Macular Degeneration .......... 150

Chapter 13
    My ministry ................... 161

Chapter 14
    An epilogue ................... 176

Bibliography ........................ 180

# List of photographs

All photographs by Kenji Konda, MSC.

Front Cover: The author in front of a copy of Salvador Dali's sculpture Dance of Time; in the background: d'Arenberg Cube, McLaren Vale, South Australia.

*Author at RSB, Knapman House, 230 Pirie St, Adelaide S.A. [p. 104]*
*Author preaching [p. 118]*
*Author using computer, with magnifier over a text (1) [p. 132]*
*Author using computer, with magnifier over a text (2) [p. 133]*
*Author preparing to celebrate Mass [p. 167]*
*Author celebrating Mass [p. 170]*

# Foreword

The author tells of his challenge to come to terms with a life-changing illness and the stresses that arose, especially when this happened late in life. For him, it means facing blindness. So he set out to understand why it happened to him and, subsequently, how to live with the impacts on his quality of life. Therefore, he began to search out the details of the disease that threatened him, and this meant finding answers but in a language that he understood. This book is a result, and it aims to pass on to others the results of his investigation so that they might be helped to understand and respond as he has. With a natural curiosity and determination, he chased down the explanations of *macular degeneration* to give an insight for those who ask: 'Why has this happened to me?'

## Foreword

In his late eighties, Fr Noel Mansfield, a Missionary of the Sacred Heart, has had a full life: a teacher for forty-five years in schools and colleges in Australia and PNG, then a change in ministry so for the last twenty-one years he has been in the Adelaide parishes of Hindmarsh/Findon and Henley Beach. In later years, he developed a ministry focused on the housebound and those in institutional care. This outreach encouraged him to write this book, as he met many who suffered this particular 'disability' with the challenges of advancing age. His motivation was to assist those who are disabled (a word that can discriminate rather than accept and assist). He has endeavoured to encourage those who seek answers to the whys and wherefores of what has happened to them. He hopes that this will encourage others to make their lives more liveable and more active, despite what seems impossible.

Noel's example has been to discover why his life has changed and what this means based on fuller knowledge of the illness by asking questions of doctors and therapists, those who have the knowledge to assist him... not just once – time and again, as he persisted to seek the best and clearest answers about his eyesight and how those responses hindered or supported him.

**Paul Cashen MSC**

# About the author

Noel Mansfield has been a professed Missionary of the Sacred Heart since 1952 and was ordained a priest in 1967. He had a long wait for his ordination due to a football injury that resulted in long-term epilepsy. So he is no stranger to being restricted in one way or another. However, this has not hindered his ministry. Most of his working life has been teaching in MSC colleges in Australia and Papua New Guinea, and the latter years in parish work. While on Sabbatical in Ireland in 2007, he was diagnosed with Macular Degeneration. As his eye disease has progressed over the years, he has realised that he may be able to support others who are suffering from Macular Degeneration. He would like to share his experience. In this sharing, he hopes to encourage people to live a full life and rise above their disability.

# Acknowledgments

While I was sitting in the church after Mass, a woman approached me and asked for prayers for her two-year old grandson who was born visually impaired with an under-developed macula. I asked her name: Raelene Edwards. I then told her that I had just completed a book on Macular Degeneration. She asked: Is there anything I can do to help? From that time, she became my proof-reader and helper with any parts that I could not manage with my poor eyesight.

Dr John Wallace, together with his wife Betty, have also assisted with their expertise in proof-reading the text. I am very grateful to my sister, Anne, for pointing out the important difference between 'disabled' and 'marginalised'. She has given me tacit permission to tell part of her story in the Introduction.

## Acknowledgments

Others who have been of great assistance include Brother Kenji Konda, MSC. The chapter on my ministry was written at his suggestion. He has also been very helpful in many other ways. His expertise in technology has been invaluable. I am grateful that he spent much time in taking the photos for this book so that it comes alive. My own MSC religious community has been encouraging. I want to thank Paul Cashen for writing the Foreword and Peter Hearn for his eagle eye able to see small mistakes.

The Macular Degeneration Foundation Australia (MDFA) has helped me to clear up some misunderstandings in response to a simple phone call.

# Introduction
# Disability and marginalisation

When the diagnosis was made that I had Macular Degeneration, my first thought was: Will I go blind? It was a scary thought for me. But it was one that I could not avoid. It is undoubtedly the reason for the title of this book.

Before we go on, there is a very important distinction that needs to be addressed. By this I refer to the meanings of the two words marginalisation and disability. We must examine what it means to have a disability and how it relates to marginalisation.

The *Disability Services Act* (1993) defines 'disability' as:

attributable to an intellectual, psychiatric, cognitive, neurological, sensory or physical impairment or a combination of those impairments, which is permanent or likely to be permanent, which may or may not be of a chronic or episodic nature, which results in substantially reduced capacity of the person for communication, social interaction, learning or mobility and a need for continuing support services.

A disability is any continuing condition that restricts everyday activities.

However, marginalisation is a deeper and broader term that covers much more than just physical or mental disabilities. When people are marginalised, we have made them feel unimportant. The synonyms I found for the term 'marginalise' made me realise the broad spectrum it takes in: undervalue, underrate, disregard, overlook, underestimate, discount, look down on, wave aside, disdain. These are just a few examples of terminologies we use when we do not value something or someone.

People sometimes look down on those with physical and intellectual disabilities, taking away their power and dignity. Furthermore, others can become marginalised and treated as of less value or importance in the community due to their ethnicity, beliefs, the colour of their skin, or their gender. They can sometimes be treated as less than normal human beings; as insignificant or worthless.

My primary intention is to convey how people can rise above their limitations and lead productive and inspiring lives. Perhaps people with disabilities are more inclined to appreciate life over those do not have disabilities. Let me reflect for a short time on some examples of people with various disabilities who have influenced my way of thinking about marginalisation.

I have observed many people with disabilities of one kind or another and have been inspired by their courage as they have faced adversity.

These people can be seen in the media and admired for what they have achieved. They did not let their disability rule their lives or prevent them from doing what they wanted to do. I will delve into who they are and how they have risen above their disabilities.

I think the first example that I admire intensely is Helen Keller. She was born on 27 June 1880, in Alabama. In 1882, she was stricken by an illness that left her blind and deaf. Beginning in 1887, Keller's teacher, Anne Sullivan, helped her make tremendous progress with her ability to communicate. Keller went on to college, graduating in 1904 with First Class Honours. She became a renowned public speaker throughout the world.[1]

---

[1] Helen Keller, 2021, available at: https://en.wikipedia.org/wiki/Helen_Keller, [accessed 7 July 2021]

When I first saw her on TV, speaking from a braille text, I could hardly believe what I was seeing and hearing. She spoke in a rather monotonous voice, but that was to be expected when one recognises that she could not hear what she was saying. What she had to say was very inspiring!

One of her well-known quotes says a great deal to me. It illustrates how her life was lived out of a deep spirituality of the heart:

> Life is either a daring adventure, or nothing.
> The best and most beautiful things in the world cannot be seen or even touched –
> they must be felt with the heart.
> Alone, we can do so little;
> together we can do so much.

Another inspirational example is Dr Justin Yerbury who featured on the ABC program *Australian Story* on 12 November 2018.[2] He began his life as an ordinary young man. He went on to

---

[2] *Australian Story* 'No Surrender: Justin Yerbury', ABC, 5 November 2018.

study Commerce at university. During this time of study, he discovered a fact that he had not taken much notice of before. While looking at his family tree, he noticed that there was a long history of Motor Neurone Disease in the family.

When he made this discovery, he changed direction in his education and began studying Science. He later became a Molecular Biologist and a world-renowned figure in Motor Neurone Disease. In a very short time, this disease began to take over his body. In 2016, he was himself diagnosed with Motor Neurone Disease and his condition began to deteriorate dramatically.

By Christmas of 2017, he was unable to breathe unassisted, and without major surgery to provide permanent mechanical ventilation, he wouldn't survive. He was determined to continue his search for a cure and spend more time with his family, so he had the operation when *Australian Story* aired in November 2018. At that time, he was in the Intensive Care Unit in hospital, struggling with post-operative complications. He remained there for six months.

Since that time there have been remarkable developments. Not only has Yerbury finally returned home, but he has also returned to his office to continue vital research into Motor Neurone Disease. *Australian Story* related more about him when they went to see him in 2018. This program caught up with him and his family to record his astonishing progress. He has gathered a team of young scientists around him to continue his research. He has not found a cure, but he has unlocked the cause of the disease. Hopefully, this will benefit later generations.

Yerbury now uses a small computer on his wheelchair and speaks by using his eyes to compose the sentences. The words come out in a digital form but at least this has allowed him to communicate freely. He is very dependent on others to assist him, yet he remains remarkably positive about his life and work.

Sure, there are many more wonderful people like Helen Keller and Justin Yerbury that I could write about; however, there is one person who is much closer to my heart. From her I have always been encouraged. I refer here to my youngest sister, Anne. Let me just say a few important things here.

Anne was born without arms. A few times I have heard her say, 'Just say it is the "Armless One"'. Despite not having arms, Anne has never allowed this to hold her back from following her calling in life. Many people have assumed that she belonged to those who were affected by the Thalidomide drug, but this is not the case. Recently, there was a program on ABC TV about people who are fighting the government for compensation on account of Thalidomide. Anne was born long before the drug came on the market. In Anne's case, as far as I know, it was a deformity that has no known cause.

I will have to leave the argument there because I do not know any more about the causes, although it was suggested that perhaps the ages of our parents may have contributed to this. Dad was in his fifties and Mum was about forty-four years old when Anne was conceived. Here I am only grasping at straws. I do not know. Others may be able to explain better.

Anne finished her schooling at Year 10 and spent the next few years working with our mother and father at home. When she was about twenty years of age, she went to Melbourne to have artificial arms fitted. This was the only place in Australia where artificial arms were being made. But there was a problem. They only dealt with people who had a single arm to be made. I remember her telling me that they didn't know what they were doing: 'They have no experience in dealing with double amputees! When they put the arms on me, I had to find out for myself how they worked. They gathered around me and took copious notes from what I was saying'.

While Anne was in Melbourne, she made the most of any opportunities to broaden her education and prepare herself for life when she returned home. She took advantage of what was on offer in Melbourne at the time. She worked with Crawford's and did courses with the company which was the leading producer of live stage shows in Australia. She learned reading for broadcasts and dramatic productions. With this new education, she hoped there might be a future for her on radio or on TV.

She then started to apply to various radio and TV stations for a job in broadcasting. Only one of these companies was prepared to take her on but with conditions. This was a TV station. They wanted her to read the weather. Here was the catch. She was to sit at the desk and use her feet not her arms.

That was the way circuses worked in the past. They used 'monsters' and 'pygmies' as draw cards, and Anne was not going to be part of this kind of circus! I would like to have been a fly on the wall to have heard what she had to say to them! I do know for sure that she walked out on the offer. Then she decided to study Social Work. Since she had not completed her last two years of secondary education, she had to go back to school to finish Years 11 and 12. After this, she studied at the Queensland University in St Lucia, graduating in 1971.

Then there was the sudden death of our mother on Christmas Day in 1969. Mum and Anne had been living in a unit in St Lucia after our father had died in 1964. They were the greatest of friends. Anne has often said, 'I lost my best friend on that day. How can I ever really celebrate Christmas again!' In fact, it set her back considerably. When she tried to complete her final year at the University, she had to give it away. She could not manage it while she was grieving but completed her studies in the following year.

After graduating, she worked in many different places. For several years, she worked with cancer patients and grieving people. This was the only time I ever heard her say that she felt inadequate and disadvantaged by not having arms. At that time, she was working at a hospital in Sydney. She commented, 'When you are with a person whose loved one is dying or has just died, you want to comfort them. The only way to do this is to put your arms around that person and hold them. Words are not sufficient on such an occasion. With artificial arms, I cannot very well hold someone tenderly'.

Despite all these difficulties, she has managed her life with seemingly great ease. She drives her own car and runs her own house, doing her own cooking and gardening. She was married and had three stepchildren. Since her husband's death, she has managed her own home and garden. One often hears the phrase 'green fingers' to describe a person who can make plants grow well. Anne has always managed to have a wonderful garden, but I tend to think of her as having 'green toes'. Her garden is always so well kept. Mostly, she uses the cheapest long-handled screwdrivers that she can buy. I can remember her husband, Ivor, talking about these screwdrivers she used in the garden. He told me on one occasion, 'If you go out into the garden, you will find dozens of screwdrivers growing there. She is always misplacing them'.

In our family, only three of us had any interest in gardening: Mum, Anne, and me. The other siblings have no real curiosity in such things. It is wonderful how this hobby has been handed down to us from our mother.

I think I have said enough about Anne to show that she is a very special person in my life. This is not the place to tell her whole life story. I have always been encouraged by her strength and determination. Yet I am not sure that I have told her enough about my deep admiration for her courage. She has been an amazing inspiration for so many people who have met and worked with her. She has always been an encouragement to me when I have faced new difficulties in my own life.

I am most grateful for the way she has shared her knowledge about the medical world that I do not understand well enough. From her background in social work (especially from working in hospitals), she holds a wealth of knowledge that I can draw upon. We have been able to share our journeys together over the telephone in recent years. She lives in Queensland while I live in South Australia.

Let me just say that Anne's courage has been an inspiration to me as I have had to accept Macular Disease as part of my life. This is my disability and I have had to cope with it in my own way. There is no way that it is going to stop me from doing the things I want to do. For sure, I cannot do things as well as I would like to, but I am determined that Macular Degeneration is not going to rule my life! There is an old saying, 'If you can't beat them, then join them'. That is how I am going to regulate my life. Macular Degeneration has now become my friend. I talk to my eyes and tell them not to be discouraged; together we will overcome any difficulty that comes along.

In September 2018, I published a book called *Dawn to Dusk, Towards a Spirituality of Ageing*.[3] One of my friends wrote a short email when he received my book in the post. He commented, 'Congratulations on your book. You are to be commended, considering your poor eyesight'. I thought this was a quaint way to express the situation. When I told another friend about this, he commented, 'He is right, you know. You have not just sat back and allowed this problem of your sight to stop you doing the things you want to do. You have accepted it and have tried to find ways of getting around the problem. You have not let it stop you!' That set me thinking. Could I share my journey with others who have Macular Disease? It may be a way of helping others who have stopped doing what they want to do. Sharing this journey that I have undertaken may encourage others to accept their lot and move on.

---

[3] Noel Mansfield, *Dawn to Dusk: A Spirituality of Ageing*, Coventry Press, Bayswater Vic., 2018.

The three people I have written about in my book have not let their disability cause them to become marginalised. They are only a few examples of extraordinary people with disabilities who have achieved remarkable feats.

I am sure you have come across such women and men in your own lives. We cannot allow ourselves to be put on the margins of society.

Hence, I have written this small book. I hope it may inspire others to own their AMD (Age-related Macular Degeneration) and refuse to become marginalised; to live a full and productive life by accepting and rising above their limitations. As I have proposed above, 'Befriend your Macular Degeneration'.

I can also see a place for this kind of book in supporting families. So many family members do not know what to do and what to say within the family setting. However, most people with AMD must rely heavily on family members and friends. So I suspect this book may be even more useful for family members than for those with the disease.

I offer it to anyone who is interested. I cannot determine who really will benefit most. I leave that decision up to you.

**Noel Mansfield MSC**

# Chapter 1
## Beginning my story

In the introduction to this book, I wrote: 'When the diagnosis came that I had Macular Degeneration, my first thought was: Will I go blind? It was a scary thought for me'. But it was one that I could not avoid because all the literature that I first read pointed to this conclusion. Hence, the title of this book sprang to mind immediately. I will speak about my eyesight as it is now, then I will go back and tell the story from the beginning. At this stage, I would like to give an account of my journey over the past ten or more years. Without being too technical, I will talk about AMD and how I have come to deal with it in my own life.

There are many articles that one can research on the computer that give a much more technical account of the disease. My object here is to show that one does not have to be held back by a physical imperfection. One can learn to live with it and make use of the various gadgets that have been developed over the years.

If my story can be of use to others, then I am grateful that I have been able to help.

## My eyesight as it is now

In this book, I am writing about my experience of living with this disease called Macular Degeneration. However, I need to say something as a prelude. I want to speak about my present condition. This book will then spell out the story in more detail while providing a brief indication of my own world as I am living it now.

You will have to read the rest of the book to see how it unfolds; to get a more complete picture of what I mean. I was hoping to have the book published earlier, but life has changed so rapidly during this year. I have had to be patient while waiting for the book to be completed and published. I have wanted to be able to explain my personal experience of Macular Degeneration.

Part of my changing world has involved dealing with various other sicknesses that have arisen in the past few months. These have held up my progress in writing, but they are part of life, and they are especially a part of getting older. Patience was needed at this time.

I am living in a new world with new people and a new home. There are so many things happening currently that I am finding it difficult to keep up with all that is going on. On top of this, the pandemic has made the whole world a much more difficult place to live in and to travel around. Let me try to give an overall picture of my own life as I am living it now. The fact that my move happened on 26 March 2020, will indicate that it was at the time of the first 'lockdown' in South Australia.

On that day, I had changed from my own little home in a small unit by myself that I had managed for many years. The change has been minimal in real terms but, in terms of my ability to get around, the story is quite different. In my small unit, I knew where things were, and I could find my way around the house and the garden. Now I live in a house with three or four others. I enjoy their company; it is good to have companions and share conversations. My room was initially upstairs but I found the stairs too hard to manage. My former residence had only one floor level. That made it easy.

Over time, I found that the exercise of climbing stairs was in fact good for me, but a new unit was already being formed on the ground floor. I moved into it in May 2020, and it is very convenient. I have a bedroom together with a bathroom all to myself and it is near an office where my computer is housed. There is also a sitting room where I can watch TV if I choose. However, my use of the TV is limited.

I have found that I do not depend on a TV because I get most of my leisure reading on my iPad and listening to the radio. I find that listening to the News on the radio is more convenient and much easier on my present eyesight. But that is only part of the story of my changed home that is attached to a set of offices in the Henley Beach Catholic Parish. This gives me more opportunity to meet up with the parishioners. Yet, it also has its problems because of my failing eyesight. Let me illustrate this briefly.

I am a priest, and while I am residing at this house, my living here does not mean that I am employed fully in the parish. I try to work at those tasks that suit my age and my capabilities. One drawback for me is my declining eyesight. Other members of the community are fully employed in the parish. My eyesight will not allow me to do all that I would like to do.

The staff members are here on a regular basis, and I am gradually getting to know them by name. They work in set places and that is important to me for remembering them. I used to remember names quite easily but now that is becoming more difficult.

On a few occasions recently after meeting parishioners, they have shown surprise and perhaps disappointment if I do not recognise them on future occasions. Some say, 'We met last week' but I do not remember them. They must remember that I am only one person while the numbers of parishioners here would be in the hundreds; I might even suggest that it could be over 1,000 parishioners. I also have late stage 'Age-related Macular Degeneration' (AMD) which makes it difficult to focus on faces. There are two forms of this disease 'wet and dry'. I have both forms and in both eyes. My right eye is badly affected, while my left eye is in much better condition. So I rely on my left eye more than my right eye.

Let me describe in simple terms what I can see and what I cannot see. I think it is illustrated well in a short article published in *Macular Disease Foundation Australia*.[4]

## What is Macular Degeneration?

It is a painless disease that causes one to lose the central part of vision. The immediate effects of it are the loss of the ability to recognise facial features. Common activities like reading or driving a car are out of the question. Straight lines become curved. If it remains untreated, it can lead to total blindness.

*Central vision*: The macula performs this task. The macula is only 5.5 mm in diameter, yet if the macular is defective, a person cannot distinguish colours and facial features, or read books and newspapers. Over the years, my own central vision has been reduced to a minimum. When I know

---

[4] Macular Disease Foundation Australia, 2020, *Annual Report*, viewed 7 July 2021.

the size and shape of a person, and get to know their voices, I can recognise them. If they happen to be in a badly lit room, then I have difficulty. If they are more than a metre away from me, then a stranger remains only a stranger.

*Peripheral Vision*: This enables one to see something that is at their side. We usually use the phrase, 'seeing out of the corner of your eye'. That is your peripheral vision. Although your macular may be impaired, you can still see the world around you without much difficulty. You can see things if you look slightly to the right or left of the object. In this way, you can engage your peripheral vision in a more active way.

Good quality sunglasses are very useful to shade your eyes from the harmful effects of ultraviolet light. Good light and significant contrast make a great difference. For example, I am presently typing on my computer using white letters on a black background. At the same time, my computer is speaking the words as I type them. Then I can have the text read back to me after I have finished a section of a chapter. I am using the program called *Zoom Text* (I will elaborate on this program later). This is only a short explanation of what is happening, yet I hope it explains the main problem I have.

**Special request**

Now that I have explained what I can see at present, and how I can see, I would like to make a special request of my friends and any others whom I meet during my ministry. This is my special request: *Please do not treat me as a little child. I will always ask if there is something I cannot do*. People are very generous in offering a helping hand. For this I am very grateful. *But please ask before you step in and take away my independence. It is something I cherish.*

I hope that my book will expand on this and make it clearer. There is a rider to this. It is always difficult to explain what is happening and how my vision is affected. All the injections and medications will not cure Macular Degeneration. They may serve to slow the progression of this degeneration, but they will not remove the underlying cause.

I hope that I can share my journey into Macular Degeneration with others. More than this, I hope it will help others to be patient with those who are vision impaired. I also hope that it can clear up some of the misconceptions that surround this disease. It is important to understand that MD is not restricted to older people. In Australia, MD generally afflicts people over the age of fifty years, but about 10% of MD diagnoses occur in younger people.

I will return to this later in the book. They are mentioned here because the term 'age-related' can be mistaken to mean that MD is restricted to older people and this is not the case. For this reason, it is recommended that all people have their eyes tested regularly by an eye professional. The sooner it is detected the better.

At this stage, I want to establish the names that are attributed to this disease. This is for two reasons:

- First, the names, and especially the acronyms have changed over the years, but Macular Degeneration has not changed. It is simply the way it is referred to, and hence I want to provide a list of these names, so the reader understands what is being talked about.

- Second, instead of using different acronyms, I want to use consistent terminology throughout the book.

ARMD (Age Related Macular Degeneration): This name is rarely used in more recent literature. It has been replaced by the shorter form AMD (Age-related Macular Degeneration). I will use this shorter name (AMD) throughout the book.

Let me pose a question: what is the difference between Macular Disease and Macular Degeneration?

Macular Disease is an umbrella term that refers to all the problems that can occur in the macula. On the other hand, Macular Degeneration is the term used as a subset of Macula Disease. It is only one of the problems that can occur in the macula. Clearly, it refers to the aging process. I was confused about this for quite some time, and it was only explained to me recently.

So why was there confusion? It seemed to me that the name given to this whole area was not explained well. In recent literature, there is more said about 'disease' than 'degeneration'. It must be recognised that MD is a 'disease', and it does not occur only in older people.

There are a couple of pieces of information that have become clearer to me only recently. So let me clarify these immediately. I was confused about the term 'macular' and 'macula'. They appeared to be used indiscriminately. Most of my reading had been done on the Internet. Here the sources are mainly American and do not make much mention of the differences, so the more I read, the more I became confused. It is so easy for the experts to make a statement because they know what they mean. But, when it comes to a lay person reading the text, it is a different story. I decided to contact the Macular Disease Foundation Australia. I am very happy to say that my confusion was soon cleared up. So in future, I will make more use of this very friendly and informative resource.

## 'Macula' and 'Macular'

*'Macula'* is the name of something. Therefore, it is a noun. The macula is a very significant part of the eye. It is that part of the eye which allows the eye to distinguish colours and shapes. It is a very tiny part of the eye measuring about 5.5 mm in diameter, and without it we are not able to see clearly.

*'Macular'* relates to degeneration; it is an adjective that describes the kind of degeneration being spoken about. Hence it becomes an adjective and is spelled with an 'r.'

Like all our body parts, there is some degeneration over the years. However, this is a disease and so must be treated as such. My own concern is to write about the disease as it occurs in older people. Hence, I will use the letters AMD when speaking about this disease because it covers all that I want to say.

Let me just add a further note of clarification. While it does occur in young people to a lesser degree, it is still the same disease. However, it must be stressed that it is much more likely to affect those aged over 50; hence the terminology 'AMD'.

# Chapter 2
# Disease and degeneration

As I heard doctors speak, they never told me plainly what the distinction was between Macular Disease and Macular Degeneration. Or perhaps it was that I was not attentive to what was being said. It could also have been that there was only discussion about Macular 'Degeneration'. I was not aware of hearing the word 'disease' being used when I first discovered I had Macular Degeneration.

Being an inquisitive person, I wanted to know what all this meant, and then share it with others. It needed to be in language that people could understand, hence I have tried to avoid too much technical language. I also wanted to write something that anyone could read and understand without too much effort. It had to be intelligible to general readers who wanted information; and technical language had to be avoided wherever possible.

It is important that this information is correct and yet simple enough for anyone who is not familiar with technical terms. I had become confused in some areas, and I am sure there are others who are just as confused as I was. So I would like to spend some time clarifying language so that any ignorance can be dispelled.

**What is Macular Disease?**

Macular Disease is an umbrella term that refers to all the various kinds of problems that may affect the human eye. There is no intention of giving a lecture on eye problems. Many technical terms are used by professionals, but this is not the place to be too technical. I do want to say something that may be helpful to people who suffer specific problems. This may also be useful for relatives and friends who need to deal with this on a regular basis. There is a great deal of ignorance about this topic. I say this from personal experience.

That ignorance can easily be overcome. This will be dealt with in another part of my story.

## What is Macular Degeneration?

Macular Degeneration comes under the umbrella term of Macular Disease; there are twenty-two different kinds of Macula Disease, and Macular Degeneration is just one of them.[5] Since Macular Degeneration is the central concern in this book, I would like to expand on it. You will notice that there is a shift from 'disease' to 'degeneration'. If there is anything wrong with the eye, it is called a disease, but degeneration leads us to another part of the human story. Degeneration is usually associated with the aging process. We are then

---

[5] Macular Disease Foundation Australia, 2021, viewed 7 July 2021.

talking about what usually happens to an aging body. The eye is part of that body. But do not be deceived; remember, younger people are also affected by Macular Degeneration.

Before I begin to tell my story, I think I need to give some general information about Macular Degeneration. In the first chapter, I made some reference to terminology. We do need to keep in mind that this is basically 'Macular Disease'. More specifically, for my purposes in this book, we need to accept that this disease generally tends to be age-related.

There is a great deal written about this disease. Some of it is easy to follow while some of it is very technical. I hope that I can avoid the latter. At the same time, I think it is also good – in fact necessary – for us all to try to understand it as well as we can. This applies especially to family members and friends who live with those who have AMD.

Let me illustrate this by an example from my own experience.

When people give me something to read, they often show a poor awareness of what a person with AMD can read. Sometimes the writing is so small that I cannot see it at all. On other occasions, I have been handed a note that is written in large letters, and I must tell the person that the writing is too large for me to read. Each person with AMD will have difficulties that are peculiar to the individual. There seems to be no general rule that covers all people.

A friend of mine who had AMD volunteered to assist at a centre in Canberra that worked with AMD patients. He remarked one day, 'People sometimes give me a note written with a large texta. I must laugh and make light of this as I say to them, 'This is too large for me to read'. That sounds very strange, yet most people think that if the print is large, it is more legible. In fact, this is not the reality. This makes sense to me because I can relate to it from my own experience. Sometimes the writing is so small that I cannot see it at all. At other times, it is so large that my peripheral vision cannot cope with it. My peripheral vision is a key to my being able to see something. In fact, it is difficult to explain to people just what I can see or can't see. It is usually better if I can write it for myself. It is only then that I know I will be able to read it when I need to.

From my personal experiences, I would like to stress the need to understand what AMD really is – or rather – how it affects the way one can see. In a recent publication from Macular Disease Foundation Australia (MDFA), I found a concise explanation of AMD, so I will quote it in full. I am sure it will be helpful to most readers.

*What is Age-related Macular Degeneration?*

The macula is the part of your eye used for sharp, central vision. You're using your macula to read this. AMD causes the macula to deteriorate, and over time leads to blurred sight and even black spots in your central vision. This makes it hard to drive, read and recognise people's faces. The stages of AMD are early and intermediate AMD, caused by the continual build-up of waste product (called 'drusen') underneath the macula. Early or intermediate AMD can sometimes progress into late AMD. Late AMD – may be atrophic ('dry') or neovascular ('wet'). Dry AMD is caused by the gradual loss of cells in the macula, leading to a gradual loss of central vision. Wet AMD is caused by new, abnormal blood vessels growing under the macula which can leak blood and fluid. Wet AMD develops very quickly and can cause rapid vision loss. Don't assume vision changes are just a part of getting older. The earlier macular degeneration is diagnosed, the better the chance of preserving your vision.[6]

---

[6] Macular Disease Foundation Australia, 2021, *Annual Report*, viewed 7 July 2021.

# Chapter 3
# The moment of diagnosis

Now I would like to go back to that moment in time and give a detailed account of what has happened over these years since that moment.

In 2007, I was on Sabbatical in Dublin, Ireland. I was enjoying the course and the company of people from all over the world. I was appreciating being away from home and meeting so many different people from very different backgrounds and cultures. We were able to get around and see many of the beautiful parts of Ireland. I had been to this country before and on each occasion, I have felt that I was 'coming home'. So I wanted to visit as much of the country as I could in the time available. My first interest was the sights of Dublin, but there were so many other parts on my agenda. I wanted to see the countryside of Ireland which has always held a fascination for me. My family origins are from this country, and I have always found myself at home there. I will return to family origins later.

During that time, my eyes were constantly sore. A group of us had been on a short tour of Cork and Killarney when I became aware that my eyesight was not as sharp as it had been even a few months before. In fact, on the first day, I almost had an accident while I was driving. That brought me up very quickly! I was travelling behind another vehicle, and it had its indicators on. But I did not see it soon enough. The man sitting next to me noticed that I was about to drive into the back of that vehicle. His quick reaction averted an accident. I am very grateful that he saw what was happening.

Later, when others suggested that I could hand over the driving to another, I willingly consented. I felt much more at home in the passenger seat than in the driver seat. That near collision was just the beginning of my journey into Macular Degeneration – though I did not know it at the time. The others in the car had recognised that I was not seeing very well. They must have discussed it amongst themselves. One of the women in the group was appointed to speak to me. I am sure they thought I would object but, in fact, I was more than happy to hand the driving over to others more competent.

When we got back to Dublin, to the Redemptorist Monastery where the Sabbatical was taking place, I told the director of the course about the problem I was having with sore eyes. He immediately offered to take me to the 'Eye and Ear' hospital in the city, to have it checked out.

At this hospital, tests were carried out and photographs were taken to determine what the problem was. After a few hours of waiting and testing, I was told to come back in another week, and they would give the results. Finally, the doctor called me in to tell me that the tests revealed a Macular Degeneration diagnosis. Interestingly, I live in Adelaide, and the 'Eye and Ear' hospital happened to be in Adelaide Street. The doctor

## The moment of diagnosis

offered to give me the first injections while I was there in Dublin. However, I was not sure if my insurance covered this treatment, so I opted to come home and have it treated in Australia.

When I arrived home in Australia, my optometrist recommended a couple of ophthalmologists. The first of his recommendations, I had been to see before. When I did see him, I was not impressed. I made an appointment with him soon after arriving home. When I had my appointment in a couple of days, he told me that he would see me in about a month. I did not feel that he had sensed my need to have it attended to as soon as possible. After all I had not come all the way home from Ireland to be told that I had to wait another month. I was not happy with this decision. The opinion I was given in Dublin was that I should start the treatment immediately.

So I went to another ophthalmologist on my list to get a second opinion. In contrast, he offered to start the treatment that week if that was what I wanted.

He asked me, 'Are you prepared to hand this over to me?' When I agreed, he booked me in for the first appointment in a couple of days. He gave me the confidence that he would listen to me and so he became my ophthalmologist for the next ten years until he retired. I will return to him later to say more about him and his approach.

Now I know that this was the correct way to deal with the disease and not to wait as the first doctor had suggested. The diagnosis was that I had 'wet' and 'dry' Macular Degeneration in both eyes. The right eye was badly affected while the left eye was relatively better.

Since I had read that Macular Degeneration was the greatest cause of blindness in Australia, I joined the Royal Society for the Blind (RSB) and shortly after that began a course in braille. I was then well into my seventies. But it is never too late to learn. My teacher was totally blind and a minister in a Protestant church. From the RSB, I learned of the various devices that are available for people who have low vision. I will return to the RSB later in the book. I simply want to acknowledge them here. There is much more that I want to say about them and how I related to them and the institutions that I visited at this time.

# Chapter 4
# The first ophthalmologist

The first doctor I went to see told me that he would see me in a month's time. In Ireland, I heard that the sooner I began the treatment the better. With that in mind, I was not impressed with the declaration that he would see me in a month's time. I was not impressed that this doctor seemed to simply put my case on the backburner.

For that reason, I decided to seek an alternative ophthalmologist and find out if I could start treatment sooner. After the first tests that showed I had macular disease in both eyes, he told me that he could start his treatment in a couple of days. This ophthalmologist was a very highly qualified man in his field. The wall of his surgery was covered with certificates to prove the point! He did most of his studies at Oxford University. Our first meeting was in January 2008, and he remained my ophthalmologist until he retired in 2018. My first visit to him was on 11 January 2008, when he confirmed that I had Macular Degeneration in both eyes ('wet' and 'dry' forms of the disease in both eyes).

Treatment began on 16 January. He took photos of my eyes and showed them to me on the computer screen. He displayed the photos on the screen for me to see immediately and he identified the 'dry' and 'wet' MD in both eyes. The right eye was quite severe and could not be treated with great success. The left eye was in much better condition. So each eye had to have its own treatment according to its condition. I felt assured that I had made the right decision.

I will not try to give names to these treatments. I simply want to speak about what happened in my own experience. Putting technical names to these treatments would only confuse the reader. If you do wish to know the medical names for each treatment, you can find them on the Internet. My interest is in telling the story of my experience of what happened at various stages.

I do not mean that the names are unimportant. Certainly, they are very important, and they are generally very expensive. For example, the injection for my left eye costs about $3,000. You can see what I mean by expensive! However, these expenses for patients are covered by the Pharmaceutical Benefits Scheme (PBS). This means that I pay only the standard set price for any medication approved by the Australian Government which at present is $6.80 per script. On the other hand, in the USA, you need to have yourself insured before you can get any one of these drugs. If you turn up to the hospital, you need to be able to pay for them before you can start treatment.

Let me say a little more about these drugs. My comments are clearly a layperson's understanding. The one used in my left eye is specifically intended to reduce the bleeding in the eye. It was manufactured for 'wet' MD. It is not a cure. It is meant to slow down the regression of the disease. Why is it so expensive? It has taken many years to develop this specific medication for one particular purpose, that is to reduce the bleeding in the eye. This bleeding is the reason for the name 'wet' MD. On the other hand, the medication used in my right eye was originally developed for treating colon cancer. After it had been developed, it was found that this medication had an important side-effect that dried up the bleeding in the eye affected by macular disease. The amount of research was consequently reduced and yet it is only partly effective.

In my case, the doctor had to reduce the bleeding in the right eye. He did this by laser treatment. He had to stop the bleeding so that this eye could be worked on. I was always grateful that he explained each step of the way and what he was going to do. This gave me even greater confidence in him.

The vision in my left eye was much better and so it was to be treated in a different way. While it cannot be improved, the treatment is intended to slow the progress. In that way I may have my vision for a longer time; the sight is quite good in the left eye in comparison to the right eye.

In Ireland, the procedure was more drawn out at the Eye and Ear Hospital in Dublin; the photos had to be taken by a technician before I went back about a week later to see what the specialist had decided. I was pleased to know that the procedure could be done more quickly here in Australia.

*8 February: More photographing of the eyes.* This showed that the bleeding had stopped, and that the retina was now more level than it had been the last time he took a photo. Then he gave me an injection to further reduce the bleeding and hopefully improve the sight. On the following visit, he was excited to tell me that there had been a real improvement. The eye was responding to the treatment!

## Getting to Know My Ophthalmologist

The treatment had now begun. Before I go into more detail about it, I would like to turn to another aspect of my experience. I wanted to know more about this man who was treating my eyes. This happened in an unusual way.

During one session, he questioned whether I was a Catholic priest. Then he told me that he had visited a Jesuit priest in London for twelve months for instruction before he could be married in the Catholic Church. I never did find out what faith he had been before he married. From various conversations, I did get to know that he was a Christian. But that was the end of what I could find out. In connection to this, he said his family went to Christmas Mass together each year. Then with a smile, and quite out of character, he told me that one of his sons had declared that he was an atheist and would not join the family at Christmas Mass.

The doctor did not really confide any more with me about his problem. However, he did tell me that he had visited the Jesuit priest again while he was on a trip to England recently. That priest is now retired and lives in Scotland. The doctor was satisfied that he had enough information and did not need to go into the topic any further. This was not something I was expecting from him; he was usually entirely professional. Personal information was not on the agenda. But I learned something about the man who was my doctor. It took me some time to get through the professionalism. I was happy that the conversation had begun. I was beginning to identify the human side of my doctor. I will return to the treatment later because it is an important part of my journey.

## The Man

My first impressions of him were of a man who knew his job and was intent on carrying it out well. However, it also appeared to me that he did not have a very good bedside manner. He went from patient to patient without pausing to get to know the person he was treating. He was very professional and far from being personal. Let me explain just what I mean by professional. He carried out all the testing: putting in the drops, taking my blood pressure, testing for glaucoma (pressure in the eyes). Then the final test was a scan of the eyes. Every procedure that was to be carried out, he did it. In other words, he was in total control. Everything was done by him. On a couple of occasions, there would be another person assisting, yet that was a rare occasion. He was the one in charge of the whole operation. I would say that he did not trust others to do things correctly. For me, that was not the sort of eye specialist that I wanted to have treating my eyes. So I set about finding a way through this professionalism and getting to know the man behind it all. I wanted to find the human being I had discovered in an earlier conversation.

My first breakthrough came when he asked me a personal question; whether I was a Catholic priest. When I affirmed that I was, he went on to ask me a very personal question referring to something that was currently happening in his life. I will not go into detail because he was seeking advice about something that was personal to him. I cannot disclose what it was as he placed his trust in me.

Let me simply say that it was the first occasion that he had mentioned anything like this. It made our future conversations more personal, and it revealed his human side. But for me it was a way through to the inner man who was my doctor. When I told him that I had experience in this area of concern for him, he shared his predicament and asked me for advice.

This became an opening for me to learn more about this doctor and his significant change of attitude. It gave me the confidence to find some new approaches; to start looking for other questions to put back to him. His approach with patients was like this – after seeing a patient, he would go straight to the front desk to give information to the secretary. The only words that could be clearly understood were… 'I will see you in so many weeks on a certain date'. Then he would pick up the next folder from the desk and without looking around or missing a beat, he would announce the name of the next patient as he strode back to his surgery. 'Mr Mansfield or Mrs Smith'. There was no greeting or any sign of welcome.

## The Breakthrough

When I was in the surgery on a later occasion, he said something about his research into a possible cure for Macular Degeneration. That was something that I had read about but had never thought that a doctor would speak about with me. In only one article have I seen a cure referred to; most information suggests that MD cannot be cured. I saw this as my opportunity and grabbed it with both hands. I began by asking, 'What is the possibility of a cure and what is happening in your research?'

To my surprise, he became a new man. I had not met this man before. He jumped to his feet and took a texta in his hand. Using a small white board in his surgery, he then gave me a ten-minute talk. He told me at what stage his research was and how his investigation was progressing; he gave a brief mention of the companies and universities that had shown interest in his research. He told me that he had identified a molecule that if it could be reversed, MD could potentially be cured. It was more than I could take in, but it was a wonderful moment for me to witness this transformed man, from purely professional to a man on a mission. This was another side of the man that I had not seen before. He was enthusiastic and so full of life as he engaged me in his thinking. At last, I thought, I have found a way to reach the man so involved in interesting research.

From that time, I knew I could capture him on this topic. It was his life. In the ten years that I was with him, I learned more about Macular Disease than I could get from any article on the Internet. But more important to me, I had come to know the human side of my ophthalmologist. From then on, I took the opportunity to ask him about everything as he examined my eyes. Our relationship changed; he was always willing to tell me about the latest breakthrough and have conversations about his work.

I also noticed that he began to take much more personal interest in his patients. His sense of humour became obvious, and he began to show that he did care about the people he treated. They were no longer just patients. They were human beings that he could help in their difficult times. I am not sure what part I played in all this; a dedicated man of science who was prepared to change his approach to his patients. Whatever the combination of factors was, I was happy to witness this transformation.

## Final procedure

Even the very final procedure – the injection into the eye – was quite different. Rather than deal with it here, I will return to it later when I speak about my next ophthalmologist. The two methods were again so different. I will try to describe them together. I hope that it will be a clearer way to speak about each method.

# Chapter 5
# The second ophthalmologist

My second ophthalmologist has his clinic in the city of Adelaide. The two men have a quite distinctly different approach. It is not for me to judge which is the better.

Personally, I know these men to be well qualified in their field of ophthalmology and they have assisted me through a very difficult period of my life. I am most grateful that they attended so efficiently to my needs.

I was sorry to lose the first doctor due to his retirement. I suppose I was sorry because I had found a man who was willing to change and be with his patients in a more human way. I had come to respect him for the way he had changed over the years. I presume that he is still doing some research in his chosen field.

My new ophthalmologist is in complete contrast and operates in a totally different way. I would like to spend some time bringing out the difference in their approaches. The first was in total control and totally professional. By this, I do not mean that the current man is not professional; they are very different in their approach to patients and procedures. I want to spend some time talking about the procedure in the clinic.

This new man has a large retinue of staff. When you go into the surgery, the procedure is quite different from the one carried out by my former ophthalmologist. This procedure occurs in stages by many different staff members. It was quite a strange new world that I was moving into.

The ophthalmologist's responsibility is to give the injections. He is obviously the one who is running the clinic, and clearly the one in charge. He is behind the planning of the operation, but he does it in such a way where he trusts his staff to do their work properly. His primary task is to see that the injections are carried out while all the preparatory and follow-up work is done by others.

**Steps in Procedure**

Let me demonstrate the various steps to make myself clear.

*Step 1*: You go to a side desk where you give your name and date of birth. Then a band is placed on your wrist. But before the wristband is attached, the attendant asks two questions: What is your full name? What is your date of birth? Only then is the wristband attached. If there is further paperwork to be signed, it is done at this stage. I am always astounded when an attendant simply puts the paperwork to be signed in front of me and says, 'Please sign this document'. I am expected to be able to read where I am to sign. This I cannot do without some help because I cannot see the line she is referring to. I must ask the attendant to show me where to sign. I am surprised that they take it for granted that I can see the line. On each occasion, I must ask for help with this task.

In a clinic that deals with patients who suffer from AMD, I would think that they would show more care in pointing out the specific place to sign. Why am I surprised? I have Macular Degeneration and so do all the others who attend this clinic. Perhaps it is just that my MD is more advanced than the other patients. But I have heard others ask the same questions that I ask. So I am not the only one who has difficulty in seeing and reading. I do not complain but try to pass it off with a laugh.

*Step 2*: You then move to the Receptionist's desk. You again give your name and show your wristband. This is simply a check to see that you have your wristband and are ready for the various procedures.

*Step 3*: You then go and sit in the waiting room to be called for the next step. After a period of waiting, a nurse calls out my name and I follow her to a room where she records various readings: blood pressure, pulse rate and temperature. Next, I am asked to read the letters on the chart. Starting with the larger letters and then moving to smaller letters until I can read no further. Then I try to read with my left eye. This is easier, but it is still a struggle. Usually, I can read about five or six lines. It is interesting that some of the nurses give me encouragement to try to read more, while others do not try to help. I know that I am more successful when I am encouraged.

I am asked to read letters on the screen. I start with my right eye, which is very poor. The nurse knows which eye is my good eye and my bad eye. She starts with the bad eye, which is my right eye. I can read only the first couple of lines if I am lucky. Finally, an eye-pressure reading is taken for glaucoma. I am always curious about these readings and ask the nurse for the results.

So I have taken more time over the task. I now know that I can read more when I do this. In this way, I have given myself more encouragement. I am getting used to using my peripheral vision to read more. It is wonderful how a little bit of encouragement helps the completion of such a simple task. And this is true even when I do it for myself!

Usually, my blood pressure readings are consistent, but one occasion stands out. There was one very different reading where my blood pressure dropped to something like 95/50. This gave concern to the nurse and to the doctor when I did get to see him. It was followed up, and, on his suggestion, after the injection, I would have it checked in the surgery. He also advised that I visit my own doctor to have it checked routinely. The only other time I had this problem was on Lamb Island in Queensland, with my sister. That was about ten years ago. I immediately went to a doctor and discovered I had an infection on my lung. It was treated there and then with antibiotics.

On another occasion, I had quite a different experience. This time, the problem was directly related to the nurse. It happened like this. The usual procedure is that the nurse marks my forehead with a texta to indicate what injections are to go into the eyes. Before she marks my forehead, she speaks out loud to indicate what she is going to do. She says: 'I will now mark an A – for Avastin – that is to be injected into your right eye'. Then she continues, 'I will mark an E – Eylea – that is to be injected into your left eye'. However, on this day, the nurse began to tell me what she was about to do. She said: 'I will now mark your right eye with an E – for Eylea'. As soon as I heard her say this, I corrected her, 'Excuse me, that is not correct. Avastin is for my right eye and Eylea for my left'. It must have been embarrassing for her when she admitted: 'I often get my left and right sides mixed up'. I have never seen her in the clinic since that day. was going to say something about it to an attendant. But I did not have to do so.

*Step 4*: After a short wait, the nurse calls me into another room. Here my eyes are scanned separately, starting with my right eye. I find this very difficult. Because the central vision in my right eye is so weak, I cannot identify the exact spot where the light is to be viewed. On some occasions, the nurse must complete the task several times. Why? I presume that I have moved my right eye without realising it. I have no way of focusing on a set point to keep my eye steady.

With my first ophthalmologist, I found this task much easier. On his machine, there were crosshairs. Even if I could not see the light clearly, I was able to keep my eyes steady by concentrating on the blank where the crosshairs would have met. I presume that this is a much more expensive machine. So I will have to do my best with what is presented to me.

When the operation moves to my left eye, the task is much easier because I can identify the light very easily with the left eye. This takes about five minutes. I am ushered back to the waiting room on the completion of Step 4. Now I wait for the doctor to call me in for the injections. All this preparatory work – or nearly all of it – is now complete. In fact, with my first ophthalmologist, all the preparatory work in Steps 3 and 4, was carried out by the ophthalmologist himself. Here they are completed by the assistants.

*Step 5*: Even in this final stage before the injections, assistants are involved. One of them calls me into the theatre and gets me to lie down. Then he or she begins by putting numbing drops in my eyes. This was done on a couple of occasions while we waited for the doctor to arrive from the next room. On the first occasion I visited him, I did not see him coming in. He is a rather short man. He came up to the back of my head and called me by name. I had not heard his voice before this, so I did not know who it was. He was just another presence in the room. Over time, I got used to his voice and I was able to respond to his greeting and his wanting to know if I was feeling well. He began by wiping my eyes with cotton wool and antiseptic. He did this so gently while at the same time asking me to keep my eyes wide open. Then he explained the procedure.

On my first visit, he asked if I would like to have both eyes injected on the same day. To me, that was a great idea. It would cut the number of visits in half. Obviously, I agreed. Since then, I have had both eyes injected on the same day. It is so much simpler and does not trouble me in any way. I have continued this from that time. He then proceeded to explain how he would do the injections. 'I will inject the left eye first and then the right eye'. This part of the procedure was over in a very short time. He then handed me a slip of paper indicating how many weeks till the next injection. I am usually given a choice of six or eight weeks between injections. While handing me the paper, he would wipe my forehead clean of the letters placed on it by the nurse.

After only a couple of visits, he began to talk about his family. He was looking forward to taking his sons on a visit to his home country to let them experience the culture there. He talked especially about travelling around the country by train. From my own experience, the trains of his country are far more modern than we know from our TV programs. He also relates very well with his staff and often has a laugh with them.

## Comparing the Two Methods

### The First Ophthalmologist

The first ophthalmologist got me to lie down on the couch. Then he positioned a circle of wire to keep my eye lid from closing. Next, he gave a small injection to numb my eye, but he later discontinued this injection after returning from a Medical Conference in the US a few years ago. He told me that they had discovered that the number of infections from the major injection was very small; the injection to numb the eye increased the risk of infection and was unnecessary. The eye had already been numbed by the drops put in the eye. I was quite pleased when the new methodology was introduced.

The simplified method was so much easier. The doctor would say, 'Look down and to the right' and the injection of Eylea or Avastin was administered into the top portion of my eye. This was the only injection I needed. Finally, he would hold up one or two fingers for me to identify. 'How many fingers can you see?' he would ask. Then he would wait for my reply. He would then sit at the desk and write out when my next appointment was to be. It could vary from six to ten weeks. Then I went back to the front desk and the attendant would give me the time of my next appointment. Any other paperwork that was to be completed was done at this time. So the complete visit took place from front desk to the doctor's surgery and back to the front desk. It was a simple method and yet it was controlled completely by the doctor.

## The Second Ophthalmologist

I was already on the couch and had been given various drops to numb the eye. All the other preparatory tasks had been completed. It was only then that I saw the doctor. The drops were administered by assistants before the doctor came into the room. It was a waiting game as far as I could tell. We were all waiting for him to complete the task. His task was to clean my eye and give the injections. He would stroll in and ask how I felt. As he usually came into the room from behind where I lay, I did not really know he was there until I became accustomed to his voice. This was disconcerting at first. But I got used to it and became more acquainted with his tone of voice. He would then take a swab and ask me to keep my eyes wide open while he cleansed them gently with the swabs. Then he told me how he was going to administer the injection. He said, 'I will deal with the left eye first and then I will deal with the right eye'. Then he went on to say, 'Look up and I will administer the injection to the left eye'. Then he took another needle from his assistant and dealt with my right eye. He would follow this with the question, 'How many fingers can you see?'

This part of the procedure was a significant change. My first ophthalmologist used to give the injection in the upper part of the eyeball. Now I had a new experience. This doctor changed the place of the injection. Instead of giving the injection in the upper eyeball, this new doctor injected into the lower portion. He would say, 'Look up', then he would inject the lower portion of the eyeball. (Having the injection in the lower part of my eye seems to be more comfortable.) The doctor would then clean my forehead of the marks that had been placed there to show which injection was to be used in that eye. When I get questioned by people about this injection, my response is usually the same. People ask: 'You mean to say that they inject a needle into your eye?' That question comes with a cringe and a sense of disbelief! But I have been doing this for over a decade now. So I hardly notice it.

Finally, the doctor would hand me a sheet of paper that showed when my next appointment was to be. Then I was taken to the front desk to make an appointment and clear up any further things that needed to be done.

**Final Payment**

The cost of the injection in the left eye is about $3,000. The injection in my right eye costs $12.50. The scan for the eyes is also part of my final payment. I pay $70 for this. Until this time, I have never questioned it nor tried to find out why it is charged though I have often wondered why this payment is made. Now I think that it should be discussed and questioned. Why is it charged and why does it differ from one clinic to another?

The question arose again recently. A few weeks ago, I was talking to a friend who comes from NSW, he told me that he pays $400 for this scan. This seemed to be an excessive amount, So I called MDFA to get some clarification on this subject. While making this call, I remembered that this foundation is a privately run and organised foundation. They depend upon the generosity of the common people. Their views will not have public backing.

I was surprised at the answer I received: 'I am sorry to tell you there is no standard payment for this scan. You pay $70. Your friend pays $400. But I have heard of payments of up to $1,000. Each doctor or clinic can charge what they want to charge'.

I was left with a big question to which I would like an answer: Why is there such a discrepancy in charges made for the same scan? There must be some authority to whom people can appeal? But who are they? There must be someone in charge of this sort of transaction. Surely it must be someone's responsibility? So far, I have no answer.

# Chapter 6

# Complications

There are only a few times when complications have caused me concern. Some have been directly connected with AMD. Others are simply part of my journey living with AMD and others are procedural problems. I think this will become clearer as I recall them. There are also some general health issues that I have experienced that are not connected to my AMD.

1. Blood Pressure: on the occasion when my blood pressure dropped to 95/50.
2. Blood Pressure: on another occasion it rose dramatically 195/150.
3. Air Bubble in my eye.
4. Nurse not able to distinguish left from right. On this occasion, I was able to correct her on the spot.

I will deal with each of these in the text as they arise.

## Blood Pressure

I have mentioned the time when my blood pressure dropped dramatically. As far as I am aware, it had nothing to do with my AMD. However, it was a concern at the time.

The first procedure occurs when the nurse takes me to an office and measures my vital signs and blood pressure. On one occasion, my blood pressure had dropped to something like 95/50. She remarked that this was rather low and needed attention. After the rest of the procedures had been completed, including the final eye injections, I was taken back to the room where my blood pressure was taken again. This time it had risen. It was still not normal. It was recommended that I go later to my own doctor to check on what should be done next. After some more tests, my blood pressure returned to normal. My doctor now keeps a close watch on a regular basis.

## Air Bubble

On this occasion, the doctor had given me the injections, and all seemed to be okay. I will try to spell out exactly what happened next. It turned out to be one of the most traumatic events that I have experienced since I began AMD treatment. In fact, I cannot remember anything that came near the fear I felt at that time. Was I really going to go blind here and now? The fear was eventually dispelled but it was an experience that I would not like to repeat in a hurry.

Soon after the doctor had left the surgery, and I was still sitting on the edge of the bed, the nurse said, 'It is all complete. You can go now'. But I continued to sit there and try to focus on him. Everything was far from complete as far as I could determine. I knew he was dressed in a black uniform. But I could not see him in a black uniform. It appeared to be a bright fuzzy blue one. So I said to him, 'As I look at you, all I can see is a blue uniform. I am not leaving this surgery until I have seen the doctor again. Something has gone wrong'. The nurse escorted me to the waiting room and said, 'The doctor will see you when he has finished with his other patient'.

After five minutes, one of the nurses came out and took the pressure on my eyes. Both eye pressures were quite high around 80 or so. She then told me to just remain seated there for about ten minutes and she'd come back again and test the eyes once more. Then another nurse came out and tested both eyes and said that they were both reasonably normal now. The pressure had gone from them.

That wasn't satisfactory. I told the nurse I was not able to see anything out of my left eye which was supposed to be my good eye. I needed to see the doctor. I was advised to wait for a while and just rest, and they would make another consultation with the doctor. The nurse told me that they would dilate my pupil and then the doctor would have another look at it. I asked her to explain to me in common language what she meant by dilating my eyes. Then one of the assistants came in and put some more drops in my eyes. They were used in the dilation of the eyes.

About ten minutes later, another nurse came to take me to the doctor's consultation room. 'Come with me and I will take you to the doctor's surgery. Just follow me'. I stood up and was trying to follow her. But she took off at such a brisk pace, there was no way I could see where she was headed. I remained standing where I was. She must've been twenty paces in front of me by then. I waited for her to come back to me. She eventually realised that I was not moving. Only then did she turn and come back to help me. She asked, 'Is everything okay? Just follow me to the surgery'. My response was simple and direct, 'No, everything is not okay. I can't see where you are. That is why I want to see the doctor. Only one of my eyes is good enough to see. I cannot see where you are going. Unless you are near me, I cannot follow you. I cannot see that far, and I do not know where you are heading. Please slow down and let me know where we are going. I cannot see more than about three paces in front of me'.

She then went on at a slower pace, but I still could not keep up with her. I simply stopped where I was and waited. I sat down. I was getting frustrated. She was not considering my sight. She could see where things were, and she knew how to get there! When we finally arrived at the surgery, I was quite concerned because I could not see out of my left eye at all. Then I noticed that there was a bubble in the left-hand side of the left eye. When the doctor arrived, he said, 'Yes you have an air bubble that has developed in the left eye, but it will go away in about 12 to 48 hours'. It went to schedule. It did go away, and things returned to reasonable normality. But from this experience, I knew what it was like to be blind in both eyes.

My general impression is that my eyesight has dropped off dramatically in the last few months. I will need to have some more advice.

# Chapter 7
# Learning Braille

When I made an appointment to begin the braille course at the Royal Society for the Blind (RSB), I was surprised when I met my teacher. He was entirely blind. He was a well-built man in his forties. He was well-dressed in a suit and tie. I suppose I should have been expecting someone like him to be my teacher. Yet, for some reason, it took me by surprise.

This first meeting was difficult for me. I was still thinking of him as a blind person. His whole outlook changed my way of thinking of him. He was moving around the room so easily. He was familiar with all the furniture and the equipment that the room contained. I noticed that the furniture was placed in such a way that there was plenty of space for movement. I presume that was done so that he would not have to negotiate furniture.

The office desk covered the whole wall on one side of the room so that there were no corners. The cupboards with the paper and other items were along another wall. Everything was in its own place. So when the teacher wanted to get something, he could open the cabinet and it would be exactly where he had placed it. It was designed for such a situation.

Over the following weeks, I was able to get to know more about him. He was a married man and a minister of religion. He made his disability appear so normal. I showed interest in his ministry and asked him about it. He was a minister in a Protestant church. However, I do not remember him telling me to which denomination he belonged.

At that time, he was teaching braille and looking for a church that would employ him. Shortly after the braille course, he moved out into a country parish in South Australia and is still there now as far as I know.

The day I met him for the first time, he had come by train and bus from his home. The use of public transport was part of his routine. He did not seem to find it complicated. He moved around with great confidence. So that put me at ease in accepting him as my teacher. It was wonderful to see his expertise with technology. Even his use of the phone was so natural. I suppose he had familiarity with all this since he was blind from birth. Yet he must have spent many hours mastering modern technology that is so diverse.

It was interesting and inspiring for me to watch him negotiate his way around the computer without having to see the screen. In fact, the screen was completely black. After all, he did not need to see it – and could not see it. He was blind. He had such awareness of the keyboard that he was able to operate everything with the keyboard alone. It reminded me of the first time I had seen someone using touch typing instead of having to look at the keyboard. The typist did not have to look for the keys but knew their position without looking. It is not quite the same but, in my imagination, I had made that connection. All this was a new experience for me.

Before I go into the lessons, I think it would be helpful to say something about the origins of 'braille'. It might also be of interest to learn more about the young man, Louis Braille.

## Louis Braille (1809-1852)

Who was this young man and why is his work so outstanding?

Louis Braille was a brave young man who took up the opportunity to give the world another way of 'seeing'. In learning more about him, I hope to use my opportunity to give something more to the world. I hope that by telling his story, I will be able to demonstrate his wonderful achievements. I hope this will become clear as the story unfolds.

I had thought of braille as an ancient method of communication. But that is not the case. It is only in the past couple of centuries that it has developed into its present form. For this reason, I would like to look at older forms of writing. In this way, we may be able to discover more about the human spirit that is not hampered by disability. Rather it is taking the opportunity as it presents itself. This is a much more positive way of dealing with blindness. However, I cannot go back to the beginning and tell the whole story. I will restrict myself to the past few centuries. If you wish to know more about the earlier forms, you will need to research it for yourself on the Internet. My interest is in researching for what is immediately of interest to me and, I hope, to those who have AMD.

Braille is named after its creator, Louis Braille, a Frenchman who lost his sight because of a childhood accident. While he was playing in his father's workshop, a tool he was using slipped and injured his eye. The damage eventually affected both eyes, resulting in his being totally blind from the age of about four years.

Braille was a very intelligent child and received a scholarship to the Institute for the Blind in Paris. He was also an accomplished musician. In 1824, at the age of fifteen, he developed a code for the French alphabet as an improvement on 'Night Writing' which was previously invented by Charles Barbier de La Serre (1767–1841) at the request of Napoleon. The 'Little General' was looking for a way of communicating at night. He wanted his soldiers to be able to communicate without having to speak so he asked some of his army intelligence officers to develop a way of communicating in the dark and in silence. The soldiers found it to be too complicated and it was never accepted by Napoleon's Army, but it became one of the foundations of braille.

Barbier introduced his concept to the blind at the suggestion of members of the French Royal Academy of Sciences. In 1821, students at the Royal Institution for Blind Youth in Paris assembled for a demonstration of Barbier's system. It was favourably received, because the older system of embossed Latin letters with its curves and straight lines was much harder for blind people to understand than the simple patterns of dots.

Barbier also provided a system by which the students could write his symbols using a special writing board and a pointed tool to make the dots. Louis Braille was at the conference when Barbier presented his findings. He recognised the value of the 'Night Writing' that Barbier had invented; however, he identified two major defects of this code. Braille realised that 'night writing' fell short as a useful tool for blind persons.

First, by representing only sounds, the code was unable to render the orthography of the words. Orthography refers to spelling of words and writing of a language. Barbier's method did not help in recognising a word and how it is spelled because it was based on sounds in the French language.

Secondly, the human finger could not encompass the whole 12-dot symbol without moving, and so could not move rapidly from one symbol to another.

## Louis Braille's Solution

This young man offered a solution and developed a completely new system over the next ten or twenty years. His first contribution was to have a set symbol for each letter of the alphabet. He was not concerned with the sound it made, but with the spelling of words. His first contribution was to use 6-dot cells and to assign a specific pattern to each letter of the alphabet. At first, braille was a one-to-one transliteration of French orthography. The second was to reduce the number of raised dots from twelve to six. Each letter is set on a series of six raised dots  three down and two across. Or it could be described as two columns of raised dots, each column having three dots in it. In this way he overcame the difficulty of the human index finger being able to cover the symbol.

Louis Braille published his system, which subsequently included musical notation, in 1829. The second revision, published in 1837, was the first small binary form of writing developed in the modern era.[7]

Soon various abbreviations, contractions, and even logograms were developed, creating a system much more like shorthand. In written language, a logogram or logograph is a character that represents a word or phrase: Chinese characters, Japanese kanji, some Egyptian hieroglyphs, and some graphemes in Cuneiform script are also logograms.

His work continued after his death. The expanded English system, called Grade-2 Braille, was complete by 1905. For blind readers, braille is an independent writing system, rather than a code of printed orthography. So it is not meant to

---

[7] See http://en.wikipedia.org/wiki/Braille.

be, in its developed form, a simple replacement for a written book. It has taken on its own form of life. In this developed form, it is what one could call 'a way of speaking' on paper.

There are variations of braille in other languages. Let me just stay with English. If you wish to know more, you can easily explore the subject on the Internet.

In English braille, there are three levels of encoding:

Grade 1: a letter-by-letter transcription used for basic literacy;

Grade 2: an addition of abbreviations and contractions; and

Grade 3: various non-standardised personal stenography.

## Some experiences

Personally, it took me some time to learn braille because my fingers were not sensitive enough. So I had to become more sensitised to the touch of the dots. I was told to use emery paper and rub this over my index finger; it did help me to feel the dots more easily.

There was a sort of breakthrough that came to me one day when I got into a lift in the city. Here I discovered that each of the levels were not only in Arabic numerals (1, 2, 3, etc.) but they were also on a panel in the lift in braille form representing each of the levels of the building. This is because of the way numbers are indicated in braille. In braille a=1, b=2, c=3 and so on. Ground level is in the form of 'g'.

I discovered this almost by accident. But I am sure that my teacher must have said something about it when we were learning numbers. One thing I know for sure is that it was a 'eureka moment' for me, like switching on a light in a dark room.

*Author at RSB, Knapman House, 230 Pirie St, Adelaide S.A.*

Now every time I get into a lift anywhere, the first thing I feel for is the 'braille sign' indicating the level. On a couple of occasions, I have been surprised that they were absent. This is not common. It is just interesting for me to search for this as my first port of call.

Of the three levels of braille, the only one that I managed to get a feel for was Grade One.

That is the one for basic literacy. I tried to move to the next level (Grade Two) with the abbreviations and contractions that accompany it. I tried it but did not stick at it long enough to get a real grasp. Now after several years away from it, I am beginning to think I need to get back to braille and learn it properly. That is a problem I must face honestly.

## Sign Language

I like to compare this way of communicating with the finger and hand motions of the people who communicate with the hearing impaired. At first, they go letter-by-letter and then they move into a faster and more fluent way of expressing themselves.

As a young man, I was staying in Brisbane with my aunt and uncle, Dulcie and Frank. Frank's brother and sister-in-law were deaf and mute. The one I saw most often was Dulcie. She had married into this family and adapted herself to their way of communicating. I admired the way Dulcie could communicate with her in-laws with sign language. She was very much at home with this form of communicating. On a few occasions, I saw her preparing food in the kitchen. It was so easy for her to make toasted sandwiches in the café that she and her husband ran in South Brisbane. At times, I saw her making these sandwiches for customers. She could carry on her task of cooking with one hand and at the same time she would be communicating in sign language with the other hand.

Many years later, when I was in the United States in 1982, signing was commonly used at conferences and public addresses. I attended a Religious Education Conference in Chicago that year and all the major addresses were signed.

Here in Australia, I had not seen it done until recently. It has become common place only in this century. To my knowledge, before the turn of the century, it was hardly used at all. I may be mistaken in this. Perhaps I was just not observant enough to recognise it.

The first time I saw it used in Australia was in the Year 2000 at an Opera in the Adelaide Performing Arts Centre. Since then, I have seen it used very regularly. When there are extremely severe weather warnings about cyclones or fires, television broadcasts are accompanied by signing. This is an important step forward for us in this country. On ABC Television nowadays, it is the norm rather than the exception.

Before I go on to describe my own method, I need to say where I got to in my attempt at learning braille. I say that deliberately, because I never did stay with it long enough to say I had mastered braille. This will be further described when I speak about my substitute for braille.

**Braille Machine – Perkins Brailler**

The first step was to use a machine that was rather cumbersome and chunky. It reminded me of the rather heavy typewriters that I first came across. But this machine was meant to transcribe letters into braille symbols. The paper that is used on this machine is much thicker than the ordinary letter paper we commonly use.

# Will I go blind?

My teacher would take me through the letters on the brailler. I was gradually able to learn the alphabet in braille. Then he would set me a task of translating a few sentences from braille into English. He would make up a few sentences on the brailler. I would take this home and spend quite some time changing the braille sentences into English. He then moved on to typing sentences in English, and my homework was to transpose these sentences into braille.

The next step was the difficult one for me. He moved the lessons into Stage Two where he taught the various abbreviations and contractions that are available. It was okay to learn them. I think that is almost the end of the story. I found this so difficult that I have not really done much with the braille I have learned so far. I had set aside a couple of days each week to learn the lesson and to do the homework. But I know that my heart was not in this. I completed the course. The next step was to practise it. Here I failed to keep up. I am now in 'no man's land' and my sight is deteriorating. I will have to return to learning braille or find an alternative.

I do not know if I will really get back to learning braille properly. I found it difficult. Now many years later, I do not have the enthusiasm nor the interest to do this. Since then, I have found other forms of technology to help get around my tasks. I have my computer, my iPad and iPhone set up so that I can use them easily. That is how I am writing and reading this text at the present without having to use braille. For me personally, this form of technology is much more helpful. I have found this easier.

However, it would be even easier if I could touch-type more confidently. I did learn it but have never really been confident. It has remained stagnant over the years. Now might be the time to get it moving again. Then I could also move to using other forms of technology, such as 'Dragon'. I did start to use it years ago but did not persist with it.

# Will I go blind?

Each person can find their own way of overcoming a difficulty. Here is my way of doing these things. Each person must adapt themselves to their own situation. I will try to describe what has been helpful to me. You must find your own way. If you find this helpful, then please feel free to adapt it and use it for yourself.

# Chapter 8

# My substitute for braille

I do not know if I will really get back to learning braille properly. I found it difficult. Now many years later, I do not have the enthusiasm nor the interest in doing this.

In about 1990, I was the Rector of a Minor Seminary, Chanel College, in Papua New Guinea near Rabaul. Someone gave us a couple of small Apple Computers. At first, they were a great mystery to me. I gradually learned to use the computer and found it very useful. It was so much easier than trying to use a typewriter.

These machines were small Apple computers, with a very small screen. However, that did not seem to worry me at the time. I had discovered a new way of communicating. It was a turning point in my life. Little did I think that it would be of much use to me. Only years later when I developed Macular Degeneration did I discover how important it would become.

**My Own Method**

When I was diagnosed with AMD, I had my computer set up so that I could read what I was writing. The program was called 'JAWS.' I persevered with this program for some years. Then I discovered that it was meant for people who are totally blind. I did not think it suited my needs. After consulting a technician at the RSB, I changed to another program called 'Zoom Text'. This is meant for people who have low vision. Since I have used this program, I have not really mastered the whole program. I have used only parts of it that suited me.

Here are the most important parts that I use regularly:

1. Black screen face with white typing
2. Text size

3. Reading the text
4. Basic Keys

There are many more parts of the program that I could use but I have restricted myself to the most useful shortcuts. I know it would be most helpful if I used the whole program but that has not been necessary, and it would be very time-consuming to learn it all. I can get along with these parts, and so I will stay with them for the present. Learning the whole program will be my next task.

### 1. Black screen face with white typing

On an ordinary computer, there is black writing with a blue background. Most difficulty is with the blue background. Most of the literature on AMD specifies that blue is a colour to be avoided. It is harmful to the human eye. If that is the case, I wonder why this colour has not been changed.

Black is the colour I have chosen; but I will need to do some modifications if there are better alternatives. I will investigate this if I think it is necessary.

At present, my computer, iPhone, and iPad are set up in this way. I have not sat down and thought it through. For the present, I am finding this set-up quite useful.

## 2. Text size

This can be changed with the use of a couple of short-cuts. I will not go into detail here. Let me make only one comment. For example, I can change fonts from larger or smaller without much difficulty.

## 3. Reading the text

As I am typing this script, I have a pair of earphones connected to the computer. As I type, I hear what is being typed and then at various times, I can listen to the whole paragraph or more if I choose. To do this, there is a restriction on what can be read back. The typing must be in Microsoft Word form. First, the text to be read is to be chosen. Then it is copied. Finally, it is read by Zoom Text.

This sounds complicated but once one gets used to the program, it is a very simple process.

## 4. Basic Keys

There are about ten of these Basic Key combinations. They are listed in the literature that comes with the Zoom Text program. It would be unnecessary to list them here. However, I would like to mention what they are for. They help the user to move more easily around the program. Once you get to know them, they become part of you.

# Chapter 9

# Blindness

In the attempt to search for a ray of light amid what we are experiencing, in our facing up to the effects of Macular Degeneration, and before proposing a few practical things that we can do about it, I wish to devote a chapter to a parable told by Jesus Christ two thousand years ago. Although this book is addressed to all people of good will, regardless of their religious convictions, the parable is one that any of us can relate to and find challenging.

For myself, I know that my Macular Degeneration has become more aggressive over the past couple of years. I am certainly not proposing a miraculous cure. I have been able to cope with the aggressiveness of this disease in my own way. I am writing this book precisely because I have been able to manage my life with Macular Degeneration. I am proposing some practical things that you might be able to do in your own life.

I also hope that by sharing my journey, you may be encouraged to live with this disability in your own way.

Let us look at this Bible passage and see what light it can throw on our human lives – and give us encouragement as we travel this road together. We do not walk alone. We travel as companions.

There are three passages in the Gospels that are related. Matthew has two blind men cured (*Matthew 9:27-32*) while Luke has a single cure (*Luke 18:35-43*). These passages may be connected but I wish to stay only with Mark's version because Mark is more relevant to the message I wish to talk about.

*Author preaching*

## Curing the Blind Beggar (Mark 10:46–52)

Then they came to Jericho. As Jesus and his disciples, together with a large crowd, were leaving the city, a blind man, Bartimaeus (which means 'son of Timaeus') was sitting by the roadside begging. When he heard that it was Jesus of Nazareth, he began to shout, *'Jesus, Son of David, have mercy on me!'*

Many rebuked him and told him to be quiet, but he shouted all the more, '*Son of David, have mercy on me!*'

Jesus stopped and said, '*Call him*'.

So they called to the blind man, '*Cheer up! On your feet! He's calling you*'. Throwing his cloak aside, he jumped to his feet and came to Jesus.

'*What do you want me to do for you?*' Jesus asked him.

The blind man said, '*Rabbi, I want to see*'.

'*Go*', said Jesus, '*your faith has healed you*'. Immediately he received his sight and followed Jesus along the road.

The healing of the blind man, Bartimaeus, is not told here to suggest that there is a cure for blindness, or one form of it in Macular Degeneration. We know that at present there is no known cure for MD. But there are ways of living with it peacefully.

Mark wrote the story so that all of us may know that we can be healed. This healing involves more than just going to doctors so that they can help those who are in need. For sure, that is part of the story, but we trust that one day there will be a break-through. Medical knowledge is always attempting to break down these barriers. On the other hand, that would be a very shallow understanding of what healing is about. This story has a much richer value than getting rid of blindness. Rather, it is told so that we can reach an understanding of the power of God in our human lives.

Let us then take the story and see its richness. This story needs to be fleshed out. Only then can we appreciate its full value in our lives.

The story begins with a statement about the day on which this event took place. It was a Sabbath Day. This was a day of rest. God completed his creation on the seventh day, the Sabbath and rested (*Genesis 2:2-3*). In recognition of this wonderful event of creation, it was demanded that all Jews should rest on this day. It was a Holy Day.

We need to recognise that Jesus' enemies were looking for something they could bring against him. So they were setting traps to catch him out. Perhaps they thought he might work a miracle on this Holy Day. In their eyes, he would be breaking the Sabbath law.

It begins in the city of Jericho in the southern part of Israel. This city is the place where many stories are told. It is on the West Bank of the Jordan River. Jesus must have passed that way on many occasions. It is, therefore, central to areas of Jesus' ministry in Israel. Let us examine some of them to see why it so fundamental to his ministry.

**The City of Jericho**

When the nation of Israel was attacking the country of the Canaanites, they came to the city of Jericho and surrounded it so they could have it for themselves. The people of Jericho thought they had their city so well fortified that they would not need to be concerned. How wrong they were!

The people of Jericho would have had a bird's eye view of the marauding tribes of Israel as they crossed the Jordan River. They would have looked on these people as mere foreigners who could not possibly capture them behind their fortified city. They trusted in their impenetrable walls.

The book of Joshua gives a detailed account of the whole story and the final fall of the walls of Jericho. Archaeologists have discovered that the story in the book of Joshua is quite incorrect. The truth is that the wall collapsed because they were faulty in their construction. These walls collapsed before the Israelites attacked. The impenetrable walls did not live up to their name. Other evidence points to an earthquake in the 6-7th Century BC.

Whatever the cause of the collapse, this city was a landmark. It remains a place of pilgrimage for many thousands of people from all walks of life.

Let us look at some of the significant stories that are connected with this city of Jericho.

## Parable of the Good Samaritan

Jesus told the story of a man who was travelling on the road from Jerusalem to Jericho. The man was attacked, beaten, robbed, and left dying on the side of the road. The story does not need to be repeated here.

The central point of the story is the contrasting responses by two religious leaders (*a Priest and a Levite*) and a Samaritan foreigner.

The first two should have known and acted differently. They were preaching one thing and denying their own preaching by the way they acted. They did not want to be defiled by the injured man's blood. They turned their backs on a man in need, a man who was injured. In contrast, a Samaritan, a complete foreigner, saw the man and went out of his way to assist the injured man. He was the only one who fulfilled the Torah, the Jewish law.

## Zacchaeus

Zacchaeus was a tax collector in Jericho. He was a very rich man, and his desire was to see Jesus. You could say that he made a kind of fool of himself by publicly climbing a sycamore tree to get a better view. Jesus called him down and invited himself to Zacchaeus' home for a meal. In response, this man gave generously to the people from whom he collected the taxes for the Roman government.

## More aboput Bartimaeus

The Gospel of Mark (10:46–52) tells of the cure of a blind beggar named Bartimaeus. He is one of the few recipients of healing whose names evangelists let us know. In Matthew and Luke, a similar story is told but he remains unnamed. In Mark's community, he had a special role and so he is named. Whatever the reason for this, it is not so important for our purposes.

My own theory is that Bartimaeus has a special role in Mark's Gospel. His story is told in connection with the imminent suffering and death of Jesus. He is also one of the few people who can give us the real identity of Jesus. He gives us a prayer to Jesus, and he especially shouts his request, and he carries out all the things that are signs of a true disciple.

Let us take each of these parts of the story and air them so the full meaning of this story is revealed.

The others in the crowd tried to keep this blind beggar out of sight and therefore out of mind. But this was the very reason that Jesus came amongst us. He came to heal our blindness. Yet we must acknowledge that Jesus was more interested in spiritual blindness than physical blindness. That is not to say that he did not cure physical blindness. He did this on more than one occasion.

At the same time, Jesus was more interested in a deeper blindness. By this I mean the blindness of those who refuse to see. He had been trying to enlighten, and, therefore, cure the spiritual blindness of the people whom he was addressing. This was particularly the leaders of the Israelite people. His own followers, including his chosen apostles, also failed to understand his message. Hence, Bartimaeus was being held up as the true disciple. He was one who really understood what Jesus was talking about. Bartimaeus had true spiritual sight.

As the story began, he could not see who was there. But he was excited and interested in knowing. When they told him that Jesus of Nazareth was there, he was obviously interested and began to shout, '*Jesus, Son of David, have mercy on me*'. This was a Messianic title and tied Jesus back to the great King David.

King David was held up as the wonderful leader of the People of God. He was also one of the most important writers of the Psalms. He was often recorded as dancing before the Lord. Though he was far from perfect in his personal life, he showed a great sense of contrition. He was also a good shepherd of his people.

Bartimaeus kept shouting: *'Jesus, Son of David, have mercy on me'*. He would not be silenced.

Jesus stopped and told the people, *'Call him to me'*. As soon as they told him, he jumped to his feet and threw his cloak aside. In doing this, he showed that he was prepared to discard all his worldly possessions to follow the call of Jesus. This man now had a new calling or vocation in life. Also, his continual shouting of his prayer showed that we must do the same. God is always listening. He will always hear us if we pray with confidence.

Note also that Jesus always wants us to state our request in our own words. He does not care if we stumble or get things wrong. Jesus wants to hear our request from our own lips. He said to the blind beggar, *'What do you want me to do for you?'*

Bartimaeus immediately responded, *'Rabbi, I want to see'*.

He called Jesus, *'Rabbi'*, that is *'Teacher'*. This recognition of Jesus as a teacher was something the leaders of Israel refused to give him. Yet this blind man could recognise it even before he received his physical sight.

Jesus then acknowledged this man's faith, *'Go, your faith has cured you'*. Without a moment of hesitation, Bartimaeus, a former blind beggar, immediately followed Jesus along the road.

While I can say that I am managing AMD in my own life, I would like to pay special thanks to my religious brothers, Missionaries of the Sacred Heart, especially here at Henley Beach. I would also like to thank all my friends in the parish who go out of their way to help me. To all of these and to my own family and friends, I thank them all from the depths of my heart. Without them I would not be able to manage my journey. Like Bartimaeus, I need support and help.

# Chapter 10
# Technical support

In this chapter, I wish to speak about technical support that is readily available. At the same time, I will restrict myself to things that I have found most helpful. There are many more organisations and other systems – some are free, and others are expensive. You will need to be careful that you choose those that offer good help without being too expensive. That is up to you to decide.

I have used only a few of the gadgets that are available. So I must restrict my comments to the things I am familiar with and that I know have worked for me. My comments will be very personal. At the same time, I wish to be helpful and set you on the right road so that you can make your own decisions.

**Royal Society for the Blind (RSB)**

From the beginning of my journey into Macular Degeneration, I have found the RSB to be most helpful and cooperative. I suppose I could say that about most of the organisations I have contacted. However, RSB was my first port of call, and it was there that I learned braille – even if not very well. That is not their problem. I have explained my difficulties elsewhere in this book.

*Author using computer, with magnifier over a text (1)*

There is one gadget that I have found most useful. I would like to recommend the desktop magnifiers that are available. These allow you to read books and newspapers. You can adjust them to suit your own needs – both in colours and in font size.

They come in various kinds. I would suggest that you visit the RSB showrooms and try them out. They are like a car. You can start at the top of the range and work down. Or you look at the kind that suits you and wait for that kind to come on the second-hand market. In that way you can save quite a deal. Or you can buy the most expensive if you can afford it.

*Author using computer, with magnifier over a text (2)*

If you wish to know more about the RSB, you can look it up on the website. They are also very helpful and friendly over the phone. You can also visit their office and find out much more information. It would be too difficult for me to write about all that they can do. In fact, they can recommend much more than I know about.

## Apple Support

If you are an Apple user, there are a couple of things that I would like to point out:

- First, there is a general number for all difficulties (1300 321 456).
- Second, there is a special number for Accessibility.

Let me say a few things about this special number for Accessibility. I will not give the number here in case they prefer me not to do so. It is a restricted line.

Accessibility is a very large part of the iPhone and iPad. It is so large that they have a special phoneline that is open all day and night (24/7). The number assists people who have hearing, visual or psychological problems. I have found it most useful when my skills fail me, or my friends are unavailable.

Some people – they call themselves my friends! – have told me that it is a special line for me because it deals with people who have mental difficulties. I will have to accept this and pass it off with a laugh.

# Technical support

When I have contacted them, I have found them most helpful and patient. I am also sure that they must sometimes get a bit frustrated with the questions I ask. Recently, I called about something on my iPhone. The woman asked what my problem was, and I immediately listed about four or five things I wanted to have a look at. She responded, 'Now you have just given me half a dozen things. Please let us deal with them one at a time!' Then we went back over them and fixed the problems.

My difficulty is that my sight will not allow me to have a written list of things to be done. I am learning that I need to slow the process down and prepare for the conversation more clearly. I need to recognise that these technicians cannot be mind-readers.

## ZoomText

Here I wish only to introduce the technology and make a couple of personal comments. Let me point out the parts of the software that I have wanted to know more about and have found most useful. I have not tried to learn the whole program. I have restricted myself to those parts of the program that give me the ability to use this technology without too much effort.

## What was I looking for in having this software on my computer?

I wanted to be able to select articles that were of interest to me and of help for my ministry. Examples of this are the various emails I receive – personal and professional. People send me emails and I want to read them without too much effort. How can I go about this?

First, I select the article (or part of the article) that I want to read. (NB The text must be in Microsoft Word form.) Secondly, I choose this article and copy it. Thirdly, on the ZT Magnifier/

## Technical support

Reader, I choose *'Tools'*. Fourthly, I choose *'background reader'*. When this is complete, the article chosen will be heard through the earphones. This may sound quite complicated but when you get used to the workings of ZoomText, it gradually becomes clearer with practice. This has taken me a few years to learn. Now I can use it easily with these same instructions. It is a game of patience! ZoomText is a powerful computer access solution that allows low vision computer users to see, hear and use everything on Windows desktops, laptops, and tablet devices. ZoomText gives you the tools to enlarge, enhance and read everything just the way you want, so that you can fully enjoy using your computer.

ZoomText is available in two product versions: ZoomText *Magnifier* and ZoomText *Magnifier/Reader*.

- *ZoomText Magnifier* provides the complete set of screen magnification tools for enlarging and enhancing everything on your computer screen

- *ZoomText Magnifier/Reader* provides all the features of *ZoomText Magnifier*, plus a user-friendly set of screen and document reading tools tailored for low vision users. ZoomText reading tools are also perfect for individuals with learning disabilities, low literacy, and other print disabilities.

Both versions of ZoomText are designed for users of all ages and skill levels and with the goal of providing independence, productivity and success at home, school and in the workplace.

I do not want to make this too complicated. I am sure that the help that is offered on the program would be better followed than my instructions.

There is one thing I am sure of: without this technology, I would not be writing this, using my computer.

## Monitoring your Vision

If you've been diagnosed with Age-related Macular Degeneration (AMD) or you are at risk, it's important to ensure you are monitoring any changes in your vision. If you notice any sudden changes, it is imperative to speak with your eye health professional (an optometrist or ophthalmologist) as a matter of urgency. It could be a sign of Age-related Macular Degeneration.

With wet (neovascular) AMD, vision changes can be sudden and severe. If this is the case, early action is key to saving your sight. Prompt treatment is crucial. If you delay treatment, it can increase the likelihood of permanent vision loss.

## The Amsler Grid

The Amsler Grid is used to monitor vision between eye exams. It is an essential and easy-to-use self-monitoring tool that detects changes in vision. These changes may include distortion (straight lines appearing wavy), blurred patches or dark patches.

However, it is important to remember that the Amsler Grid should never replace regular eye examinations. The only way to diagnose Age-related Macular Degeneration is to have an eye examination, including a check of the macula, by an optometrist or ophthalmologist.

### What does an Amsler Grid look like?

An Amsler Grid is a card that shows a grid pattern with a dot in the centre. Amsler Grids are available free of charge from Macular Disease Foundation Australia. Your Amsler Grid will come with a magnet on the reverse side, so you can stick it to the fridge.

### How do I use an Amsler Grid?

When using the Grid, it is important that you test one eye at a time. This allows potential issues to be identified in each individual eye. So for example, if you have Age-related Macular

## Technical support

Degeneration in one eye only, you may not realise it. That's because the eye with the better vision will compensate for the lack of vision in the eye with AMD.

1. If you use reading glasses, you should wear them when using an Amsler Grid.
2. Hold the Grid at your normal reading distance, that's usually about 30cm from your face, in a well-lit room.
3. Cover one eye with your hand and focus on the centre dot with your uncovered eye.
4. Repeat with the other eye.

If you see wavy, broken, or distorted lines, or blurred or missing areas of vision, you may be displaying symptoms of AMD. Contact your eye health professional immediately. Prompt treatment may save your sight.

It is important to note that if you have already been diagnosed with AMD, you'll be monitoring for changes in what you usually see. Is it more blurred than usual? Do the lines appear more wavy than usual? Are missing areas of vision larger than usual? If this is the case, early action and prompt treatment are crucial to saving your sight.

## How often should you use an Amsler Grid?

If you have been diagnosed with Age-related Macular Degeneration, use the Amsler Grid daily. If you are over the age of 50, monitor your vision with an Amsler Grid weekly [MDFA 2021].

This is very important information. Let me make a couple of personal comments. About fifteen years ago, an Amsler Grid was shown to me by a friend who is a pharmacist. I could not make head nor tail of it. Perhaps I already had some signs of AMD. Since that time, I have not really found it helpful. I am sure that it must have some value for many people. Only while I have been writing this book, have I begun to discover its value. At the same time, I cannot work out the pictures that go with the distortions that are supposed to take place. It remains a mystery for me. If it is of help to you, then please do not be put off by these negative comments; that is my experience.

# Chapter 11
# Some questions

**Do these injections hurt?**

People often ask me if these injections hurt. In my experience, I can say that I have felt only the slightest inconvenience on a couple of occasions. I have been treated now for twelve years. So to the question, I would answer NO!

However, a friend of mine who also gets injections has told me that he really feels them. I do not mean just 'feeling' but 'real pain'. As a result, he has to go back to the specialist and have a contact lens on his eye for about a week. Only then can he bear the pain. When I heard him say this a few years ago, I asked my first ophthalmologist about this pain. His comment was straight forward, 'If there is any pain felt, then the injection is not being administered properly. There should not be any pain. I would suggest that your friend report him to the medical authorities. Perhaps he might even think of changing his ophthalmologist. Certainly, there should be no pain'.

**Does it frustrate you not being able to see clearly or to read?**

Recently, when I was speaking with my friend, he commented to me that he could read when he removed his glasses and held the book up close to his face. He was able to read quite easily – even small print. It was only then that I realised that my problem was much more severe than his. So I contacted the MDFA to ask about this. They were very helpful, and I received this reply.

There are three distinct stages of AMD:

1. Early AMD
2. Intermediate AMD
3. Late AMD
    a. Dry (atrophic) AMD
    b. Wet (neovascular) AMD

As you can see above, the late stage of AMD can be divided into two types: dry or wet. This reply was very helpful.

For further information, you can visit: https://www.mdfoundation.com.au/about-macular-disease/age-related-macular-degeneration/stages-of-amd/ [MDFA 2021]

Personally, I am unable to read an ordinary book. I can read this print on the computer, but I have had it adjusted for me so that I can read it. I use white writing on a black background. This can be changed with Zoom Text technology. I can see it well enough, but I also have the earphones that read the text to me.

Of course, there is always a wish to be able to read. I could get frustrated. But that is not going to improve the situation. This book is about living with disability and not getting discouraged. What is the point of this? We all must accept our limitations or disabilities. We all must accept the aging process and the problems it brings. Getting frustrated will not help us in any way.

## Memory

I am blessed with an ability to remember things. I know that there are some in my family who say that I am forgetful. I can accept this. It is the truth. I am old enough to remember my distant past. There are times when I tell the same story many times. I must accept this as a fact.

However, when I am speaking about memory, I mean the ability to remember and recall quite large sections of texts, I can learn things by heart. I find this a great blessing. I can remember large passages of text and be able to comment on what I have just spoken about.

## What is the purpose of the white cane?

It assists me in walking and helps me to recognise uneven places on the footpath. It is not a walking stick. People can see it quite easily and often ask me if they can help. I do know that some drivers speed along and do not take any notice of the cane. On one occasion, I made a definite sign with my cane. The driver pulled up very smartly! I learned a lesson from that incident. I need to make the cane obvious to drivers. Since that occasion, I have not had problems.

When I purchased a white cane from the RSB, my first reaction was a sense of embarrassment when using it in public places. It has taken me time to get over this feeling. In one sense, I would like to be able to move around without the cane. On the other hand, I know that it is something I need to get used to and get over feeling self-conscious.

I know I would like to be able to move around easily, but that is something of my past. It is an assistant – even a friend – and that is how I must begin to treat it. I have found that making fun of the cane has made it easier. Over recent times, I have been thinking of various names I could call my friend. My first thought was to call it 'WC'; that did not seem to be an appropriate name for a friend. So I have settled for 'Whitey.' I am still getting used to speaking to my friend by name. Time will tell if this name sticks. Then again, if it is a friend, it will become easier.

I do know that my friend warns me of bumps in the footpath. I tend to be a fast walker. Now I have slowed down, I have avoided tripping and falling. I have even found myself talking to the cane as a friend; this makes the whole situation easier. When it has helped me to recognise a bump, I need to thank it as a companion. This sort of thing may sound ridiculous, but I have to find ways around the problem. And this is my way.

# Chapter 12

# Diet for AMD (Age-related Macular Degeneration)

**Suggestions**

The first ophthalmologist I went to see on a regular basis made some suggestions about diet. He gave me some simple ideas. I will try to recall them here. Then I will add some more recent material that has appeared.

The first thing he recommended was eating vegetables that have dark green leaves, such as spinach and similar leafy vegetables. He said, 'The darker the green, the more valuable they would be'.

## Diet for AMD (Age-related Macular Degeneration)

Then he went on to specify some other foods that were useful. He gave them in a mixed form. I took note of them: oranges, nuts, bananas, tuna (or any oily fish.) I wrote these down and used them. However, I decided that I needed to arrange them in a form that was easier for me to remember.

So I arranged them into a pneumonic to assist my memory. The pneumonic was BONT.

B: bananas
O: oranges
N: nuts
T: tuna

This has been very useful over time. But since then, there has been more literature about 'The Best Diet for AMD'. This does not diminish the validity of the above. Yet it does add more to the picture. I will spend some time on this to explain it to the best of my ability.

The most useful article I have found is, *'The Best Diet to Fight off Macular Degeneration'* published in 2018 by Joyce Hollman. This entry was posted in Eye Health and tagged Natural and Organic Foods posted on 15 November 2018.[8] Hollman began the article by speaking about a black spot that you might experience when you wake up. No kind of washing of your face and eye will remove the spot. From my own experience, I have never had a black spot that I could detect in my eyes. For sure, my eyesight is blurred and has become ever more so over the years.

The idea of a black spot is interesting. From my own experience of AMD, I am not sure that this is the best way to describe it. There seems to be another way of describing what I can see. I may be wrong, but I would like to express it in words. The black dot seems to me to arise from these printed pictures. This would seem to arise from the various pictures that are printed. This is the description that comes from the many

---

[8] Eye Health: Natural and Organic Foods posted on 15 November 2018 [Eye Health: 2018].

articles that have pictures in them. The only way that such a disease as MD can be described is in the appearance of a rough black dot or hole. I am really struggling to explain what I can see or not see.

My comment comes from my actual experience of suffering MD over more than twelve years. At this present time, I am at a loss to find other words to describe what I am trying to say. There is one thing I am sure of: 'black dot' does not do it justice. So I would like to describe it from another perspective. I know that I feel that I would like to have my eyes scrubbed to see more clearly. I have often thought to myself if only I could scrub my eyes, I would be able to see better. But I also know that this is not possible. The problem is from within the eye and unfortunately it has nothing to do with the external functions of the eye.

Let me express it in yet another way. Let me compare it to driving a car when the windscreen is foggy. When the windscreen becomes fogged up, you can clean the window. The difference is that you cannot remove the fog or blur from your eyes when you have MD. With this disease, your vision is constantly blurred or foggy.

There is another point that I must add. I have written this in another chapter, but it bears repeating. The foggy vision comes when you try to identify faces or subjects that require you to see defined objects. Your macula identifies these.

On the other hand, the world around you is the normal world. Or rather, I should say, it appears that way. Why? Because your peripheral vision appears to give you the whole picture. It is only when you look directly at someone's face and engage your macula that the difference becomes obvious.

Let me repeat something I have written above:

- Your macula picks up faces, straight lines and colours.
- Your peripheral vision gives you an overall view.

## Reviewing old research

Until now, MD was considered an incurable disease. But recent research has totally changed that and given new hope. I do not think that it will happen in my lifetime; however, we must cling to hope. The human spirit thrives on hope.

We can all be like the blind beggar, Bartimaeus, on the side of the road. We can shout our request and know that it may one day be answered. Bartimaeus lived in hope and was rewarded.

Good research can uncover things that have been known, but for some reason, the results of one investigation went unnoticed for a long period of time. There were once two large research projects in Europe that escaped notice for a long period. It was only when they were looked at from a different perspective that they revealed a hidden secret. A large group of researchers throughout the European Union went back over research and discovered an open secret. Let us spend some time looking at these studies.

The first of these was the Rotterdam Study that evaluated the disease risk in people aged 55 years and older. The other study was the Alienor Study that assessed the association between eye disease and nutritional factors in people aged 73 years and older. When re-examining these studies, the European researchers discovered that people who followed a strictly Mediterranean diet were 41 percent less likely to develop Macular Degeneration than those who didn't follow the diet. Another factor was probably even more important. The researchers found that eating only a few of the foods in a Mediterranean diet had no effect. It was the combination of the foods in the diet that prevented MD.

Another European study confirms this news. Doctors at the University of Coimbra in Portugal analysed diet questionnaires from 883 people aged 55 or older. Of those who adhered to a Mediterranean diet, only 39% had MD, as compared to 50% for those who did not adhere to this diet. Two interesting trends emerged in this study: eating five ounces of fruit a day and drinking more caffeine both made the odds against developing MD even better.[9]

I am still at a loss to know why this is so. It seems so strange that caffeine has this effect. I can accept the fruit content in the result, but I do not understand why caffeine has this effect. I would like someone to explain this to me. So far, I have not heard a good rational answer.

---

[9] Eye Health: Natural and Organic Foods posted on 15 November 2018 [Eye Health: 2018].

## How to eat a Mediterranean Diet

You've read quite a bit regarding the wonders of the Mediterranean Diet. Its staple foods are fish, nuts, olive oil, fruits and vegetables, seeds and nuts, and whole grains. This style of eating could save more than your sight! It beats inflammation and that can help keep your brain young and save you from heart disease.

## The Macular Degeneration Cookbook

The *Macular Degeneration Cookbook* by Ita Buttrose and Vanessa Jones is published by Macular Degeneration Foundation Australia. The first foreword is written by Ita Buttrose, AO, OBE, Australian of the Year 2013. She writes: 'Since becoming the patron of Macular Disease Foundation Australia in 2005, I have become aware how widespread the disease is and how much ignorance there is about it in the community'.

As one who has suffered from this disease for many years, I know from firsthand experience just how much ignorance there is. This is one of the reasons I have struggled to present this book to any Australians who are concerned or even not concerned. Ignorance is a terrible obstacle. Yet it can be overcome. The second foreword is written by Vanessa Jones. She loves her life as a chef and knows that if this can help people with MD, she is happy to be part of the team.

The Introduction is written by ophthalmologist Dr Paul Beaumont, AM. He introduces the topic: 'What do we know about Macular Degeneration?' He writes a very pithy summary of the subject.

He does it in a couple of pages that are not filled with technical jargon and well worth a read for those who are wanting to become familiar with this subject.

## Will I go blind?

There must be many more studies and papers published on this topic of MD. I hope I have covered most of the relevant articles. There is no need for me to name them all. Many are available on the Internet. I have selected studies and articles that made sense to me and did not go into unnecessary jargon that is hard to follow.

# Chapter 13
# My ministry

Recently, one of my confreres asked, 'Why don't you write something about your ministry as a priest?' The question was an obvious one. And yet it was so close to me that I did not think to say anything about it. This question has stirred up a few things that I have taken for granted over the years.

I was ordained a priest in 1967. After more than fifty years as a priest, there is much I could say about my ministry. I do not intend to tell the whole story. My intention is to relate how I minister now that I have advanced Macular Degeneration.

When I told someone that I was writing a book about my experience, that person said, 'How can you write a book when you cannot see?' I hope I will be able to explain this in the following pages.

Since my ordination, I have ministered in various parts of Australia and Papua New Guinea. While ministering as a priest, I have spent many of these years teaching in classrooms. Over this time, my ministry has been varied and rewarding.

At the heart of my ministry has always been my priesthood. While I spent most of my time in classrooms, on my weekends and during holidays, I had the opportunity of ministering in a variety of parishes. This has taken me to a multitude of towns throughout Australia and PNG. While I was in the Solomon Islands, there was a revolution. The people decided to break away from mainland PNG. It was an interesting time to visit the Solomon Islands because many of the students at Chanel College were from these islands. It was also quite an experience to be there while the Revolution was just beginning.

These travels brought me into contact with people of all walks of life. I have also ministered in the Pacific Islands of Nauru and Kiribati especially on the island of Barnaba. These latter places were only short stays. Yet they were significant for me.

I would like to tell just one story of my short stay of a couple of months on the island of Barnaba. This island was known for its rich deposits of phosphate. It is situated approximately halfway between Nauru and Kiribati. This is in the middle of the Pacific Ocean and on the Equator. The effects of climate change have been dramatic for the inhabitants. They have now moved off the island and bought another island to the south. As far as I know, the island is no longer inhabited.

It was the Sunday before Christmas when I celebrated my first Mass there. The people did not know who I was. I thought I should introduce myself to the congregation. Not knowing the language, I had to find out how to say my name in their own language. I went to the resident

Catechist, who was fluent in English, and asked him how I should say my name. I asked him, 'How do I say 'Father'? He told me it was 'Te Tama.' I asked him how to say 'Noel' and he replied, 'Noere.' I found that in their language, there are only sixteen letters in the alphabet five vowels and eleven consonants. They did not have an 'l', so they could not say 'Noel.'

Now I had my introductory remark prepared. When I stood before the congregation, it was a different story. I confidently stood in front of the people and told them my name. However, I failed to remember that they had been a French colony and their pronunciations and vocabulary were of French origin. When I introduced myself to them, I said, 'My name is Te Tama Noere', and I was surprised to see and hear their reaction. They were sitting on the floor of the church. When I made my announcement, they rolled around the floor and laughed heartily.

At first, I thought I had made some blunder in what I had said. There could have been a mistake in my pronunciation. Then I realised what they had heard me say. What I said was correct, but what they heard me say was different, 'My name is Father Christmas'. When I thought back over my words and their reaction, I was able to join in their laughter, and it was a wonderful lesson to me. Since that time, I have often told people that my name is Father Christmas. They are a beautiful, fun-loving people, with a great sense of humour. Their singing is out of this world! They made the celebration of Mass into a wonderful sense of the sacred.

## Retirement

At this point of time in my life, I have retired to some degree. Living in Adelaide, much of my ministry has been with the elderly. Now that my sight is greatly depleted, I have had to look at new ways of ministering.

What do I mean by 'retirement'? In the previous sentence, I said, 'I have retired to some degree'. When I began to write about this, it became obvious to me that retirement can be taken in various ways. I have spent much of my time writing books. I enjoy doing this. So I will continue to do so as long as I can. Then when I tried to spell out the different ministries I have been involved with, it became clear to me that I am still quite active in the parish. You will see what I mean when you read the following pages.

Let me spell out some of these ways that I can minister even with low vision.

## Celebrating Mass

My main preparation these days is centred on the readings that are set for the day. Today is Monday of the sixth week of Easter. I will use this as one example of how I approach these readings and then how I use them throughout the celebration.

The readings for today are as follows:

First: Acts of the Apostles, 16:11–15
Responsorial Psalm: 149:1–9
Gospel: John 15:26 to 16:4

*Author preparing to celebrate Mass*

I do not attempt to read these to the people. In fact, the people are only too willing to help in reading. My task is to have prepared some thoughts from these readings beforehand. The first reading was about St Paul preaching to the women at the place of prayer outside the city. He was travelling through what is modern-day Turkey. One of the women in the group was named Lydia. She was a devout woman and the Lord opened Lydia's heart to accept what Paul was saying. She was baptised there and then at that place. She was a very wealthy woman who was in the purple dye trade. She then invited the disciples to come to her home and she would not take any excuses. Obviously, she was a very strong woman in the community.

The Psalm speaks of God's people: 'The Lord takes delight in his people' (Psalm 149:4).

Finally, in the Gospel from John, Jesus promised his disciples the gift of the Spirit of Truth. It is this Spirit that will lead his followers into all truth. Just as Lydia's heart had been opened to receive Paul's message, so the Spirit of Truth will lead Jesus' followers into all truth.

The prayers and the Preface of the Mass can be quite difficult. I try to take a couple of thoughts from the readings and weave these into the prayers and Preface. I have discovered that the simpler the thoughts expressed here, then the more successful they are. A few of my confreres have helped me in getting these prayers into a simpler form.

**Eucharistic Prayer 2**

Let me introduce a few thoughts about the Eucharistic Prayer. It is the central prayer of the Catholic Church. In fact, it is a summary of what we believe. It is really a song of praise and thanksgiving to God for all that he has done for us through his Son, Jesus. In the first few centuries, there was no set form for these prayers. Celebrants composed the prayers as they went along. The most important was an invocation of the Holy Spirit over the gifts of bread and wine.

*Author celebrating Mass*

There were two significant early prayers. One was composed by Pope St Leo and the other by St Hippolytus. In his introduction, Hippolytus said that his prayer was not to be learned by heart. Rather it was simply giving a possible text for the prayer. Any celebrant could use their own words as long as they followed the basic outline.1 This has given me great encouragement. Learning long passages of any sort of text has never been a problem for me. When I know that this is part of our tradition, I feel a greater freedom in composing the prayers needed to celebrate. When I am celebrating the Mass, I know Eucharistic Prayer 2 by heart. Now I know that I do not have to stick to the exact wording in the book, I am able to add other thoughts that are appropriate for the occasion. This has made me feel 'at home' with the people and the celebration.

**Concelebration**

Sometimes I concelebrate with other priests. In this kind of celebration, the priests share parts of the Eucharistic Prayer. Recently, I had an interesting experience. When the main celebrant had finished his part of the prayer, he moved aside and allowed me to continue with the next part. But it has not happened quite so smoothly on many occasions. Why? The priest who handed over to me pointed to the prayer where I was to continue. The difficulty was that I could not see where he was pointing. His finger and the printed page were a blur for me. This meant to me that he did not understand that I could not read the text.

How could we overcome this difficulty? It would be easier for me to continue without having to have the place pointed out. One suggestion has been made and it makes sense. Instead of pointing to the text, it would be more helpful to say the first few words where I am to follow. I also need to speak to the other priests and find out exactly where they want me to continue my part of the prayer. Perhaps the first step would be to talk to them about what the difficulty is and how I think it can be overcome. Such a conversation would assist us all in understanding Macular Degeneration. After all, that is the very reason I am writing this book.

## Celebrating with the Elderly Parishioners

I have been invited to celebrate Mass once a month with the elderly parishioners in Henley Beach. This is a wonderful occasion to meet up with them. We have this Mass in the afternoon. So the people do not have to be up and about too early. They feel quite relaxed. After Mass, there is time to have a tea or coffee with them. It is a good way for me to meet them. I can walk around and speak to them. My eyesight is not good enough to help remember all of them. But that does not get in the way. I will gradually get to know more of them by name.

## Mass at the Retirement Village

This retirement village has Mass every couple of months. It follows the same routine as the Mass at Henley Beach Parish. A group of parishioners gather in a small room at the village. They have all the necessary things ready for Mass. Usually, there are about ten people who gather. I think the important thing for them, as it is for the elderly at Henley, is that they feel welcome and at home. As Pope Francis has so often remarked, 'The elderly must not feel rejected or discarded'.

**Bible Talks**

Now there has been another invitation. I have been invited to give some talks on the Bible. This is a wonderful occasion to be able to share what I can with people. These talks will not be formal. They will be an occasion to share knowledge rather than impose it. I would hope that I can speak simply about the Word of God. Hopefully, they will feel comfortable enough to ask me questions about the Bible. By this I mean, I hope they will come to have a more personal relationship with their Lord Jesus.

## The Sacrament of Reconciliation

The Sacrament of Reconciliation is offered to the people at various times. On Saturday morning, I take my turn in this on a regular basis. All these things are still in their infancy. Yet I can already sense that some of their deepest needs are being met. Let us hope and pray that the Spirit of the Lord will be there to guide us.

# Chapter 14

# An epilogue

William Shakespeare had a very deep understanding of the human person. He suggests we all pass through various stages in our lives. There is no easy way to know them all. Yet all of us go through them whether we like it or not. It is a journey from being a baby through the stages until we reach old age. Then we return to a stage that is not very different from babyhood. It is a journey from birth to death.

We may be able to bypass some of these stages in our own lives, yet he gives an understanding of the human spirit that is part of us all. Not all these characteristics can be seen in everyone. Shakespeare's expression of these stages in his speech should give us pause to think about ourselves. These stages are quite revealing.

In this wonderful speech in his play *As You Like It*, we may be able to recognise ourselves even in a shadowy form. He calls these the 'Seven Stages of Man'. There is no suggestion that I am going to write a commentary on this speech. However, I would like to allow this speech to be read in the context of our own lives with all its limitations, and at the same time to savour our lives as a gift. Each one of us will take a message for ourselves. May your message be received with gratitude.

The speech expresses so well our human personality in all its quirky developments. I would like to see what it can tell each one of us about our disabilities and our strengths.

A few parts of the speech can also be associated with the aging process. Clearly, my intention is to focus on the final stages. But we also need to recognise that the other stages are part of our lives. In doing this, I acknowledge that not all of us are afflicted with this degeneration. I also want to acknowledge that MD is not restricted to the elderly.

The final stage is one that recalls our disabilities. It is a moment in time that is the lot of us all. So I invite you to take your place on this stage of life and enjoy your moment of glory.

### All the World's a Stage

And all the men and women merely players;
They have their exits and their entrances,
And one man in his time plays many parts,
His acts being seven ages. At first the infant,
Mewling and puking in the nurse's arms;
And then the whining schoolboy, with his satchel
And shining morning face, creeping like snail
Unwillingly to school. And then the lover,
Sighing like furnace, with a woeful ballad
Made to his mistress' eyebrow. Then a soldier,
Full of strange oaths, and bearded like the pard,
Jealous in honour, sudden and quick in quarrel,
Seeking the bubble reputation
Even in the cannon's mouth. And then the justice,

## An epilogue

In fair round belly with good capon lined,
With eyes severe and beard of formal cut,
Full of wise saws and modern instances;
And so he plays his part. The sixth age shifts
Into the lean and slippered pantaloon,
With spectacles on nose and pouch on side;
His youthful hose, well saved, a world too wide
For his shrunk shank; and his big manly voice,
Turning again toward childish treble, pipes
And whistles in his sound. Last scene of all,
That ends this strange eventful history,
Is second childishness and mere oblivion,
Sans teeth, sans eyes, sans taste, sans everything.
(*As You Like It*: Act II Scene vi)

# Bibliography

ABC 2018, *Australian Story No Surrender: Justin Yerbury*, television program, ABC, 5 November.

All the world's a stage, 2021, available at https://en.wikipedia.org/wiki/All_the_world's_a_stage, [accessed 7 July 2021]

Braille, 2021, available at http://en.wikipedia.org/wiki/Braille, [accessed 7 July 2021].

Buttrose, I & Jones, V, 2014 *Eating for Eye Health: the Macular Degeneration Cookbook*, New Holland Publishers, Australia.

*Disability Service Act 1993* (Government of South Australia)

Eye Health: Natural and Organic Foods posted on 15 November 2018 [Eye Health: 2018].

# Bibliography

Helen Keller, 2021, available at https://en.wikipedia.org/wiki/Helen_Keller, [accessed 7 July 2021]

Hippolytus of Rome, 2021 available at https://en.wikipedia.org/wiki/Hippolytus_of_Rome [accessed 7 July, 2021]

Macular Disease Foundation Australia, 2020, *Annual Report*, viewed 7 July 2021, https://probonoaustralia.com.au/wp-content/uploads/2010/08/2020-Annual-Report.pdf

Macular Disease Foundation Australia, 2021, viewed 7 July 2021, https://www.mdfoundation.com.au/about-macular-disease/age-related-macular-degeneration/stages-of-amd/

www.ingramcontent.com/pod-product-compliance
Lightning Source LLC
Chambersburg PA
CBHW011317080526
44588CB00020B/2732